Merry
TEATIME

WHITE CHOCOLATE–PEPPERMINT
SCONES WITH PEPPERMINT CREAM,
page 39

Merry TEATIME

Christmas Delights to Sip & Savor

83PRESS

Hoffman Media
2323 2nd Avenue North
Birmingham, Alabama 35203
hoffmanmedia.com

ISBN #979-8-9874820-9-4
Printed in China

ON THE COVER:
Red Velvet–Cream Cheese Bundt Cake,
page 116

Contents

Introduction

A MERRY AFTERNOON TEA IS A WONDERFUL WAY TO CELEBRATE THE CHRISTMAS SEASON and makes a unique gift for those hard-to-buy-for friends and relatives. From charmingly cozy and intimate gatherings to splendidly elegant and grand fêtes, an array of possibilities abounds for celebrating this most wonderful season with those you hold dear. Whatever your desired theme or aesthetic, this curated compilation of ten festive table settings and 93 recipes will yield an abundance of inspiration for hosting your next holiday teatime, whether in the afternoon, as is the norm, or as a brunch on Christmas morning.

Traditional tea foods in this collection are intermingled with creative twists on classics and include menus suited to children and those who are young at heart. For the health-conscious, there are plenty of tasty vegan and low-glycemic recipes from which to choose. If you're hosting guests who follow a gluten-free diet, our "Recipe Index" (page 134) will prove quite helpful. To minimize last-minute stress, tips for making food in advance are included when feasible. Expert tea pairings ensure that every sip complements the flavors of the fare, course by course, and our "Tea-Steeping Guide" (page 130) provides essential information for preparing the perfect pots of tea for guests to truly savor.

Whether the celebrations are casual or elaborate or something in between, hosting a tea party during this jubilant time of year is a marvelous way to express your love and appreciation for the special people in your life and will certainly make their holiday season, and yours as well, especially merry and meaningful.

Holiday
GATHERING

The
MENU

SCONE
Earl Grey–Pineapple Scones
with Earl Grey Cream

Fancy Darjeeling Tea

SAVORIES
Caprese Canapés

Crab & Corn Vol-au-Vents

Curried Duck & Mango
Tea Sandwiches

Imperial Yunnan Black Tea

SWEETS
Ambrosia Cakes

Cranberry & Cherry–Topped
Cheesecakes

Raspberry-Anise Linzer Cookies

Nutcracker Black Tea

Tea Pairings by Simpson & Vail
800-282-8327 | svtea.com

Invite friends and family to enjoy afternoon tea at a table set with the traditional colors of Christmas.

"Christmas gives us an opportunity to pause and reflect on the important things around us." —DAVID CAMERON

Earl Grey–Pineapple Scones
Makes approximately 12

Imparted with the citrusy flavor of bergamot from the Earl Grey tea leaves and the sweet notes of dried pineapple, these delicious, cream-based scones are wonderfully balanced and delightfully unique for the holidays.

3 bags Earl Grey black tea*, divided
1 cup boiling water
½ cup chopped dried pineapple
2½ cups all-purpose flour
⅓ cup granulated sugar
1 tablespoon baking powder
1 tablespoon fresh lemon zest
½ teaspoon fine sea salt
6 tablespoons cold unsalted butter, cubed
¾ cup plus 3 tablespoons cold heavy whipping cream, divided
½ teaspoon vanilla extract

• In a 2-cup heatproof bowl, place 1 tea bag. Pour 1 cup boiling water over tea bag, and let steep for 5 minutes. Remove and discard tea bag. Add chopped pineapple to hot tea, and let sit for 5 minutes to rehydrate fruit. Drain fruit well, and let cool.
• Preheat oven to 375°. Line a rimmed baking sheet with parchment paper.
• In a large bowl, whisk together flour, sugar, baking powder, lemon zest, and salt. Whisk in contents of remaining 2 tea bags**. Using a pastry blender or 2 forks, cut butter into flour mixture until it resembles coarse crumbs. Stir in pineapple.
• In a small bowl, stir together ¾ cup plus 2 tablespoons cream and vanilla extract. Add to flour mixture, stirring until mixture is evenly moist. Working gently, bring mixture together with hands until a dough forms in the bowl. (If mixture seems dry and won't come together, add more cream, 1 tablespoon at a time. Dough should be very firm.)
• Turn out dough onto a lightly floured surface, and knead gently until smooth by patting dough and folding it in half 3 to 4 times. Using a rolling pin, roll out dough to a scant 1-inch thickness. Using a 2-inch cutter dipped in flour, cut as many scones from dough as possible, rerolling scraps as needed. Place scones 2 inches apart on prepared baking sheet.
• Brush tops of scones with remaining 1 tablespoon cream.
• Bake until edges of scones are golden brown and a wooden pick inserted in centers comes out clean, 18 to 20 minutes. Serve warm.

RECOMMENDED CONDIMENTS:
Earl Grey Cream (recipe follows)
Orange marmalade

*If using loose-leaf tea, replace each tea bag with 1 heaping teaspoon dry tea.
**If tea leaves are large, crush them with a mortar and pestle.

Earl Grey Cream
Makes approximately 2 cups

Lusciously creamy and divinely decadent, this tea-infused condiment presents stiff competition for beloved clotted cream, and Earl Grey lovers might say it's even better.

1 cup heavy whipping cream
4 Earl Grey tea bags*
2 tablespoons confectioners' sugar

• In a small saucepan, heat cream until steaming and bubbles appear around edge of pan. Remove pan from heat and add tea bags. Cover pan, and let steep for 5 minutes. Remove tea bags, squeezing out tea-infused cream. Transfer steeped cream to a covered container, and refrigerate until very cold. (Overnight is best.)
• In a deep bowl, beat together cold cream and confectioners' sugar with a mixer at high speed until thickened and creamy. Use immediately, or cover and refrigerate for a few hours until needed.

*If using loose-leaf tea, replace each tea bag with 1 heaping teaspoon dry tea.

Caprese Canapés
Makes 12

A classic salad is turned into a lovely finger food in these simple-to-prepare, bite-size canapés that are picture-perfect for a festive gathering.

6 slices firm white sandwich bread, frozen
1 tablespoon extra-virgin olive oil
½ teaspoon dried Italian herb seasoning
⅛ teaspoon garlic powder
⅛ teaspoon fine sea salt
12 thin slices Campari-style tomato
12 fresh mozzarella pearls
12 fresh basil leaves
Garnish: ground black pepper

• Preheat oven to 350°. Line a rimmed baking sheet with parchment paper.
• Using a 1¾-inch fluted round cutter, cut 12 rounds from frozen bread slices, discarding scraps. Place bread rounds on prepared baking sheet. Using a pastry brush, brush bread rounds with olive oil.
• In a small bowl, stir together Italian seasoning, garlic powder, and salt. Sprinkle mixture evenly over bread rounds.
• Bake until bread rounds are lightly golden brown and crisp, 8 to 10 minutes. Let cool completely. Store in an airtight container for up to a couple of hours.
• To assemble canapés, blot tomato slices on paper towels to remove excess moisture, if necessary. Place a tomato slice, a mozzarella pearl, and a fresh basil leaf on each bread round.
• Garnish with black pepper, if desired. Serve immediately.

1/8 teaspoon ground black pepper
1 cup unsalted vegetable stock*
1 teaspoon Worcestershire sauce
2 teaspoons grainy Dijon mustard
1 tablespoon fresh lemon zest
2 teaspoons fresh lemon juice
2 tablespoons chopped green onion
1 tablespoon chopped flat-leaf parsley
2 tablespoons diced pimientos
1 tablespoon heavy whipping cream
1 (6-ounce) can white lump crabmeat, drained
1/2 cup frozen baby yellow and white corn kernels,
   thawed
Garnish: paprika and chopped parsley

• Preheat oven to 425°. Line a rimmed baking sheet
with parchment paper.
• Place frozen pastry shells, evenly spaced, on prepared pan.
• In a small bowl, whisk together egg and 1 tablespoon
water to make an egg wash. Brush tops of pastry shells
with egg wash, making sure egg wash does not run
down sides of pastry shells.
• Bake pastry shells until golden brown, 18 to 20 minutes. Let cool for 5 minutes before removing center of
tops and soft pastry underneath.
• Meanwhile, in a medium sauté pan, melt butter over
medium-high heat. Add shallot; reduce heat to medium-
low and cook, stirring occasionally, until shallot is tender,
approximately 5 minutes. Whisk in flour, salt, and pepper.
Whisking constantly, cook until a roux forms or mixture is
lightly browned, 2 to 3 minutes. Whisk in vegetable stock
gradually until combined and mixture begins to thicken
and become creamy. Whisk in Worcestershire sauce,
mustard, lemon zest, lemon juice, green onion, parsley,
pimientos, and cream. Taste and adjust seasonings, if
necessary. Gently stir in crabmeat and corn, and let mixture heat through. (Stir crab as little as possible so that
crabmeat does not shred.) Keep pan covered over very
low heat until ready to fill pastry shells. Divide mixture
among pastry shells. Serve immediately.
• Garnish with paprika and chopped parsley, if desired.

*Decrease salt to 1/4 teaspoon if using salted vegetable stock.

MAKE-AHEAD TIP: Crab mixture can be cooked a day in
advance, placed in a covered container, and refrigerated.
Reheat over very low heat in a covered pan or in a double
boiler over simmering water, stirring very little to not break
apart crabmeat. Bake pastry shells just before serving time.

Crab & Corn Vol-au-Vents
Makes 6

*These toothsome puff pastries with a hollow center, known
as vol-au-vents, serve as mouthwatering vessels for a
creamy and flavorful crab-and-corn filling. While fresh
jumbo lump crabmeat can certainly be used, we opted for
the less expensive canned variety.*

1 (10-ounce) package frozen puff pastry shells
1 large egg
1 tablespoon water
2 tablespoons unsalted butter
2 tablespoons finely chopped shallot
2 tablespoons all-purpose flour
1/2 teaspoon fine sea salt*

Curried Duck & Mango Tea Sandwiches

Makes 9

The unexpected flavor duo of duck and mango star in delectable ways in this tasty tea sandwich that additionally comprises roasted cashews, fresh chives, and piquant watercress on brioche bread.

1 teaspoon olive oil
2 (7.5-ounce) boneless duck breasts
¼ cup mayonnaise
2 teaspoons white wine vinegar
½ teaspoon curry powder
¼ teaspoon fine sea salt
⅛ teaspoon ground black pepper
¼ cup small diced fresh mango
2 tablespoons chopped roasted cashews
1 tablespoon finely chopped red bell pepper
1 tablespoon finely chopped celery
½ tablespoon finely chopped fresh chives
1 tablespoon Major Grey's chutney
6 slices brioche sandwich bread
½ cup watercress
Garnish: chopped red bell pepper and watercress sprigs

• Preheat oven to 400°. Line a rimmed baking sheet with foil.
• Brush a medium sauté pan with olive oil. Preheat over medium heat for 3 minutes.
• Using a sharp knife, score duck skin in ¼-inch intervals, being careful not to cut into breast meat. Rotate breast and score again, making a crisscross pattern. Place duck skin side down in sauté pan, cover, and cook for 10 minutes. Turn duck over and cook for 2 minutes.
• Transfer duck, skin side up, to prepared baking sheet, place in oven, and roast for 13 minutes. Remove from oven, and let rest until cool enough to handle.
• Remove and discard skin from duck. Coarsely chop meat. Place meat in the work bowl of a food processor, and pulse until finely chopped. (Don't over-process, or meat will be gummy.)
• In a medium bowl, stir together meat, mayonnaise, vinegar, curry powder, salt, and black pepper. Stir in mango, cashews, bell pepper, celery, and chives until combined.
• To assemble sandwiches, spread a very thin layer of chutney onto 6 bread slices. Arrange watercress in an even layer over chutney on 3 bread slices. Spread a thick, even layer of duck salad over watercress. Top with remaining 3 bread slices, chutney side down, to make 3 whole sandwiches. Using a serrated bread knife in

a gentle sawing motion, trim and discard crusts from sandwiches. Cut each sandwich into 3 equal rectangles. Serve immediately, or cover with damp paper towels, place in a covered container, refrigerate, and serve within 2 hours.
• Just before serving, garnish with chopped red bell pepper and watercress sprigs, if desired.

MAKE-AHEAD TIP: Duck salad can be made a day in advance, covered, and refrigerated until needed.

Ambrosia Cakes

Makes 12

A sophisticated spin on the traditional Southern fruit salad, this version, which is afternoon tea–approved, incorporates the familiar flavors of the dish, including oranges and coconut, and transforms them into a sumptuous confection worthy of gracing a fabulous Christmas fête.

½ cup unsalted butter, softened
1 cup granulated sugar
1 tablespoon fresh orange zest
2 large eggs
1¼ teaspoons orange extract
⅛ teaspoon vanilla extract
1½ cups cake flour
1½ teaspoons baking powder
⅛ teaspoon baking soda
¼ teaspoon fine sea salt
¼ cup whole milk
¼ cup sour cream
Creamy Orange Curd (recipe follows)
Coconut-Mascarpone Frosting (recipe follows)
Garnish: unsweetened shredded coconut flakes and
    fresh orange zest

• Preheat oven to 350°. Spray a 15¼x10¼-inch rimmed baking sheet with cooking spray. Line baking sheet with parchment paper and spray again.
• In a large bowl, beat together butter, sugar, and orange zest with a mixer at medium-high speed until light and fluffy, approximately 3 minutes. Beat in eggs, one at a time. Beat in extracts.
• In a medium bowl, whisk together cake flour, baking powder, baking soda, and salt.
• In a small bowl, stir together milk and sour cream. Add flour mixture to butter mixture in thirds, alternately with milk mixture, beginning and ending with flour mixture, scraping down sides of bowl as needed. Pour batter into prepared pan, smoothing top with a spatula. Tap pan on countertop several times to level batter and reduce air bubbles.
• Bake until edges of cake are golden brown and a wooden pick inserted in center comes out clean, 12 to 14 minutes. Let cool completely in pan on a wire rack. Wrap pan securely with plastic wrap or foil and freeze for 2 hours or up to a day.
• Using a 2-inch round cutter, cut 24 rounds from frozen cake. Place cake rounds in an airtight container with layers separated by wax paper. Let thaw completely.
• To assemble cakes, spread an even layer of Creamy Orange Curd onto 12 cake rounds. Top each with a remaining cake round.
• Place Coconut-Mascarpone Frosting in a piping bag fitted with a large open star tip (Wilton#1M). Pipe a rosette of frosting on top of each cake.
• Just before serving, garnish with coconut and orange zest, if desired.

MAKE-AHEAD TIP: Cakes can be assembled and frosted a day in advance. Store in an airtight container in the refrigerator. For best flavor, let cakes come to room temperature and garnish with orange zest and coconut flakes just before serving.

Creamy Orange Curd

Makes approximately 1 cup

This easy-to-make curd gets its marvelous creaminess from butter that is stirred in a piece at a time. Use as a filling or a topping, or serve alongside a warm batch of scones.

4 large egg yolks
¾ cup granulated sugar
2 tablespoons fresh orange zest
⅓ cup freshly squeezed orange juice
¼ cup unsalted butter, cut into 4 pieces

• In a medium bowl set over a pan of simmering water, whisk together egg yolks and sugar until smooth. (Make sure bottom of bowl is not touching water.) Whisk in orange zest and juice. Cook until thickened, approximately 8 minutes, stirring constantly. (Mixture should coat the back of a metal spoon at the end of cooking time.) Remove bowl from heat. Stir in butter, a piece at a time, until melted and incorporated. Transfer orange curd to a covered container. Refrigerate until cold and use within a week. Stir before using.

Coconut-Mascarpone Frosting

Makes approximately 2 cups

A combination of heavy whipping cream, sugar, coconut and vanilla extracts, and mascarpone cheese results in a sweet concoction that is carefully placed atop each Ambrosia Cake in the form of a beautiful rosette.

1 cup cold heavy whipping cream
3 tablespoons confectioners' sugar
¼ teaspoon coconut extract
⅛ teaspoon vanilla extract
1 (8-ounce) container mascarpone cheese,
   stirred to loosen

• In a deep bowl, beat together cream, sugar, and extracts with a mixer at high speed until thickened and creamy. Beat in cheese at medium-high speed just until incorporated, being careful not to overbeat. Use immediately.

Cranberry & Cherry–Topped Cheesecakes

Makes 16

With a chocolate cookie crust on the bottom and a healthy dollop of chilled Cranberry-Cherry Compote on top, these petite and heavenly cheesecakes are dressed up for the season in both appearance and taste. No special equipment is required—just an 8-inch square baking pan.

1 (9-ounce) package chocolate wafer cookies
   (24 cookies)
5 tablespoons unsalted butter, melted
½ cup plus 3 tablespoons granulated sugar, divided
2 (8-ounce) packages cream cheese, softened
2 tablespoons heavy whipping cream
½ teaspoon vanilla extract
2 large eggs
Cranberry-Cherry Compote (recipe follows)
Garnish: fresh rosemary sprigs

• Preheat oven to 350°. Spray an 8-inch square baking pan with cooking spray. Line with a double layer of parchment paper, letting edges hang over sides of pan to use as handles. Spray parchment paper with cooking spray.
• In the work bowl of a food processor, pulse together 24 cookies until very finely crumbled.
• In a medium bowl, stir together cookie crumbs, melted butter, and 3 tablespoons sugar until well combined. Press mixture firmly into bottom of prepared pan to create a level layer.
• Bake until set, 10 to 12 minutes. Place pan on a wire rack and let cool completely.
• In a large bowl, beat together cream cheese, remaining ½ cup sugar, heavy cream, and vanilla extract with a mixer at high speed until combined and creamy, scraping down sides of bowl as needed. Beat in eggs, one at a time, until thoroughly combined. Pour batter into prepared pan, smoothing with an offset spatula.
• Bake until cheesecake is set and slightly puffed but with some jiggle, 30 to 33 minutes. Place pan on a wire rack and let cool completely. Wrap pan securely with plastic wrap or foil and freeze for 4 hours or up to a day.
• Lift cheesecake from pan using parchment paper handles. (Run a knife around cheesecake edges, if necessary, to loosen.) Place cheesecake on a cutting surface. Using a long sharp knife, trim and discard rough edges from cheesecake. Cut cheesecake into 16 squares by pressing firmly downward to create clean cuts, running knife under hot water, and wiping clean between each cut. Place cheesecake squares in a single layer in an airtight container and refrigerate until thawed and ready to serve.
• Just before serving, spoon a small amount of cold Cranberry-Cherry Compote onto each cheesecake square. Garnish with fresh rosemary sprigs, if desired.

Cranberry-Cherry Compote

Makes 1¼ cups

A wonderful mixture of sweet cherries, tart cranberries, lemon juice, and a dash of minced rosemary produces the ideal cheesecake topping that would be equally great on all sorts of sweet or savory fare.

1 cup frozen sweet dark cherries
2 cups fresh cranberries
¼ cup granulated sugar
2 tablespoons water
1 tablespoon fresh lemon juice
⅛ teaspoon finely minced fresh rosemary
⅛ teaspoon almond extract
⅛ teaspoon vanilla extract

- Using a sharp knife, cut frozen cherries in half.
- In a medium saucepan, stir together cherries, cranberries, sugar, 2 tablespoons water, lemon juice, and rosemary. Bring to a boil over high heat, stirring constantly. Once mixture boils, reduce heat so that mixture briskly simmers, stirring frequently. Cook until fruit softens and mixture thickens, 8 to 10 minutes. (Consistency should be that of fruit preserves.) Stir in extracts. Let cool slightly before transferring mixture to a covered container. Refrigerate until cold and use within 2 days.

Raspberry-Anise Linzer Cookies
Makes 30

Perfectly dusted with a layer of confectioners' sugar to resemble snow, these scrumptious and charming Linzer cookies encapsulate a fruity filling. We used raspberry preserves, but any other jam that pairs well with the licorice notes of anise would work well, too.

1 cup unsalted butter, softened
1 cup granulated sugar
1 large egg
½ teaspoon vanilla extract
3 cups all-purpose flour
1½ teaspoons baking powder
1 teaspoon ground anise
½ teaspoon fine sea salt
¾ cup raspberry preserves
Garnish: confectioners' sugar

- Preheat oven to 350°. Line several rimmed baking sheets with parchment paper.
- In a large mixing bowl, beat together butter and sugar with a mixer at high speed until light and creamy, approximately 3 minutes. Beat in egg and vanilla extract until incorporated.
- In a large bowl, whisk together flour, baking powder, anise, and salt. With mixer at low speed, gradually add flour mixture to butter mixture, beating just until dough comes together.
- Place half of dough between 2 wax paper sheets. Using a rolling pin, roll dough to a ⅛-inch thickness. Transfer dough and wax paper to a rimmed baking sheet. Freeze for 15 minutes. Repeat with remaining dough.
- Working with one dough sheet at a time, remove dough from freezer and discard wax paper. Turn out dough onto a lightly floured surface. Using a 2-inch fluted round cutter dipped in flour, cut 60 rounds from dough, rerolling scraps as necessary. Place rounds 2 inches apart on prepared baking sheets. Using a 1-inch fluted round Linzer cutter, cut and discard centers from 30 rounds.
- Bake until edges of cookies are light golden brown, 8 to 10 minutes. Transfer cookies to wire racks, and let cool completely. Store at room temperature in an airtight container with layers separated by wax paper.
- Just before serving, spread each whole cookie with preserves. Top each with a cutout cookie, flat side down. Dust cookies with confectioners' sugar sifted through a fine-mesh sieve. If desired, fill centers with more preserves.

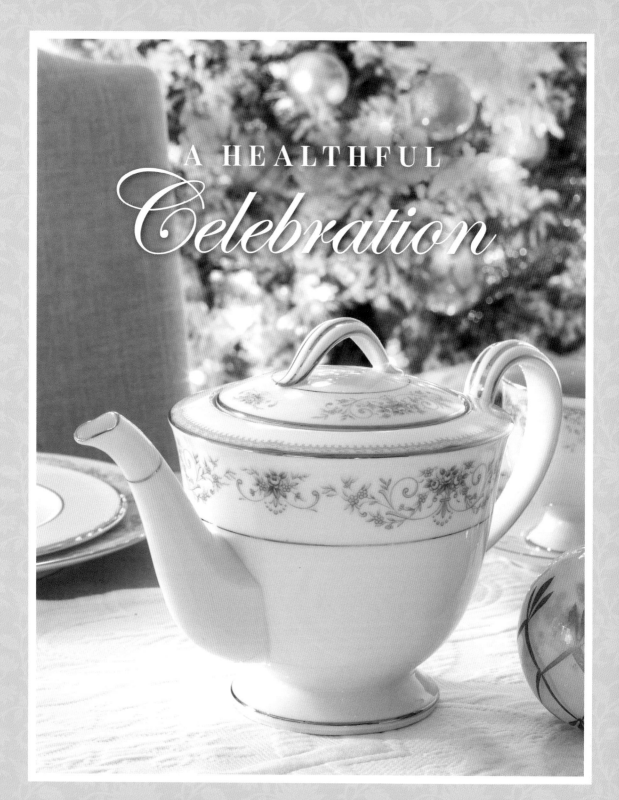

A HEALTHFUL

Celebration

The
MENU

SCONE
Sugar-free Almond Scones

Winter Spice Black Tea

SAVORIES
Curried Red Grape, Pecan &
Chicken Salad Tea Sandwiches

Smoked Salmon &
Asparagus Canapés

Zucchini, Feta & Chive Quiche Bites

Tung Ting Oolong Tea

SWEETS
Peanut Butter Cookie Logs with
Peanut Butter–Cream Cheese Topping

Cherry-Almond Thumbprint Cookies

Pomegranate-Chocolate Tartlets

Full Moon Spice Black Tea

Tea Pairings by The Boulder Tea Company
303-817-7057 | boulderteaco.com

*Treat those who must follow
a diabetic-friendly diet to a
Christmas teatime filled with
tasty, low-glycemic goodies.*

Sugar-free Almond Scones
Makes 12

Replacing granulated sugar with a diabetic-friendly alternative allows guests to enjoy these delightful scones that pay homage to classic almond sugar cookies.

2½ cups all-purpose flour
⅓ cup granulated sugar substitute*
2½ teaspoons baking powder
¾ teaspoon fine sea salt
½ cup cold unsalted butter, cubed
¼ cup toasted sliced almonds
½ cup cold whole milk
2 large eggs, lightly beaten, divided
1¼ teaspoons ginger paste
1 teaspoon vanilla extract
¾ teaspoon almond extract
12 whole blanched almonds

• Preheat oven to 375°. Line a rimmed baking sheet with parchment paper.
• In a large bowl, whisk together flour, sugar substitute, baking powder, and salt. Using a pastry blender or 2 forks, cut butter into flour mixture until it resembles coarse crumbs. Gently stir in sliced almonds until incorporated.
• In a medium bowl, whisk together milk, 1 egg, ginger paste, vanilla extract, and almond extract. Add milk mixture to flour mixture, stirring until a dough begins to form. Working gently, bring mixture together with hands until a dough forms.
• Turn out dough onto a lightly floured surface and knead gently until smooth by patting dough and folding it in half 3 to 5 times. Using a rolling pin, roll out dough to a ¾-inch thickness. Using a 2-inch round cutter dipped in flour, cut 12 scones from dough without twisting cutter, rerolling scraps as needed. Place scones 2 inches apart on prepared baking sheet.
• Gently press a whole blanched almond into the top of each scone. Freeze for 15 minutes.
• Brush tops of scones with remaining 1 egg.
• Bake until scones are lightly browned, 14 to 16 minutes. Remove from oven and let cool on baking sheet for 10 minutes before serving.

We used Swerve Granular sugar replacement.

RECOMMENDED CONDIMENTS:
Clotted cream
Sugar-free raspberry jam

Curried Red Grape, Pecan & Chicken Salad Tea Sandwiches

Makes 18

Chicken salad is a classic teatime savory. This interpretation incorporates curry powder, red grapes, pecans, celery, and sweet onion and is served on sprouted grain bread. While the onion is certainly optional, we think it adds a lovely depth of flavor.

2½ cups finely chopped cooked chicken breast
½ cup quartered red grapes
¼ cup finely chopped celery
3 tablespoons toasted chopped pecans
2 tablespoons finely chopped sweet onion (optional)
½ cup plus 3 tablespoons mayonnaise, divided
½ cup sour cream

1 teaspoon curry powder
¾ teaspoon fine sea salt
⅛ teaspoon ground black pepper
12 slices sprouted grain bread*
½ cup chopped fresh Italian parsley

• In a medium bowl, stir together chicken, grapes, celery, pecans, and onion.
• In a small bowl, stir together ½ cup mayonnaise, sour cream, curry powder, salt, and pepper until well combined. Add mayonnaise mixture to chicken mixture, stirring until well combined.
• Spread remaining 3 tablespoons mayonnaise in an even layer onto bread slices. Spread a thick, even layer of chicken salad onto 6 bread slices. Cover each with a remaining bread slice, mayonnaise side down, to make 6 whole sandwiches.

• Using a serrated bread knife in a gentle sawing motion, trim and discard crusts from sandwiches. Cut each sandwich into 3 equal rectangles, creating 18 tea sandwiches.
• Using hands, press chopped parsley onto exposed edges of chicken salad. Serve immediately, or cover with damp paper towels, place in a covered container, and refrigerate for a few hours until serving time.

*We used Food for Life Ezekiel 4:9 Original Flourless Sprouted Grain Bread.

MAKE-AHEAD TIP: Chicken salad can be made up to a day in advance, stored in an airtight container, and refrigerated.

Smoked Salmon & Asparagus Canapés
Makes 18

Blanched asparagus spears wrapped with pieces of smoked salmon are delectable snacks on their own. Place them on petite toasts slathered with a tarragon-infused cream cheese spread for elegant canapés that are sure to impress.

1½ ounces cream cheese, softened
1 tablespoon heavy whipping cream
1 teaspoon chopped fresh tarragon
½ teaspoon fresh lemon zest
⅛ teaspoon ground black pepper
18 thin spears fresh asparagus, trimmed
3 ounces smoked salmon
18 petite toasts
Garnish: chopped fresh tarragon

• In a small bowl, stir together cream cheese, heavy cream, tarragon, lemon zest, and pepper until well combined.
• Fill a large pot halfway with water. Bring water to a boil. Add asparagus and boil until bright green, approximately 1 minute. Using tongs, carefully remove asparagus and immediately submerge spears in an ice bath until cooled.
• Using a sharp knife, trim asparagus into 2-inch pieces from top of spears. Pat asparagus pieces dry with paper towels.
• Divide cream cheese mixture among toasts, spreading in an even layer.
• Using a sharp knife, cut salmon into 18 equal pieces. Wrap a salmon piece around an asparagus piece and place diagonally on top of cream cheese layer on a toast. Repeat with remaining salmon pieces, asparagus pieces, and toasts.

• Garnish with fresh tarragon, if desired. Serve immediately.

MAKE-AHEAD TIP: Cream cheese mixture can be prepared up to a day in advance, placed in an airtight container, and refrigerated. Let come to room temperature before using. Asparagus pieces and salmon pieces can be prepared up to a day in advance, placed in separate airtight containers, and refrigerated until needed.

Zucchini, Feta & Chive Quiche Bites
Makes 24

These vegetarian crustless quiche bites are assembled and cooked in the wells of a mini muffin pan.

1 teaspoon olive oil
2 cups (¼-inch) diced zucchini
½ cup crumbled feta cheese, divided
2 tablespoons chopped fresh chives
3 large eggs
1 cup heavy whipping cream
½ teaspoon fine sea salt
¼ teaspoon dried thyme leaves
⅛ teaspoon ground black pepper
Garnish: crumbled feta and chopped chives

• Preheat oven to 350°.
• Spray a 24-well mini muffin pan with cooking spray.
• In a medium nonstick sauté pan, heat olive oil over medium-high heat until it shimmers. Add zucchini and sauté until lightly charred, stirring occasionally, 1 to 2 minutes. Reduce heat to low. Cover pan and steam zucchini, 2 to 3 minutes. Divide zucchini among wells of prepared muffin pan.
• In each well, place approximately 1 teaspoon feta cheese and approximately ¼ teaspoon chives over zucchini.
• In a 1-quart liquid-measuring cup, whisk together eggs, cream, salt, thyme, and pepper until blended. Divide mixture evenly among prepared wells of muffin pan.
• Bake until quiches are set and slightly puffed, approximately 12 minutes. Let cool slightly in pan. Carefully remove quiches from pan and place on platter.
• Garnish with crumbled feta and chives, if desired. Serve warm.

Peanut Butter Cookie Logs
Makes approximately 40

Adorned with a decorative topping made from peanut butter and cream cheese, these pretty cookies have surprisingly few ingredients, yet are absolutely delectable and sugar-free. Because the dough for these cookies is quite thick, a large and sturdy cloth piping bag is a must for piping the dough into individual logs.

1 cup no-sugar-added smooth peanut butter
1 large egg
⅔ cup granulated sugar substitute*
½ teaspoon baking soda
½ teaspoon vanilla extract
¼ teaspoon fine sea salt
Peanut Butter–Cream Cheese Topping (recipe follows)
Garnish: chopped, salted, roasted peanuts

• Preheat oven to 325°. Line a rimmed baking sheet with parchment paper.
• In a large bowl, beat together peanut butter, egg, sugar substitute, baking soda, vanilla extract, and salt with a mixer until smooth and dough holds its shape, 2 to 3 minutes. (Dough will be thick.)
• Transfer dough to a large cloth piping bag fitted with a ½-inch round tip (Wilton #1A or Ateco #806). Pipe dough (squeezing bag with force for dough to come out) into approximately 40 (1¼x½-inch) logs onto prepared baking sheet. Using fingers, gently press down on dough logs until they are ¾-inch wide. Freeze for 10 minutes.
• Bake until cookies are set, 8 to 10 minutes. Let cool completely.
• Place Peanut Butter–Cream Cheese Topping in a piping bag fitted with an open-star tip (Wilton #21). Pipe topping in swirls onto cooled cookies. Garnish with peanuts, if desired. Serve within 2 hours.

We used Swerve Granular sugar replacement.

MAKE-AHEAD TIP: Cookies can be baked a few weeks in advance, cooled completely, placed in an airtight container, and frozen. Let thaw at room temperature before piping with topping.

Peanut Butter–Cream Cheese Topping
Makes approximately ¾ cup

This three-ingredient topping comes together quickly and is decadently delicious and oh-so pretty piped on log-shaped peanut butter cookies.

¼ cup no-sugar-added smooth peanut butter
4 ounces cream cheese, softened
2 teaspoons granulated sugar substitute*

• In a medium bowl, beat together peanut butter, cream cheese, and sugar substitute with a mixer at medium-high speed until smooth, 2 to 3 minutes.

*We used Swerve Granular sugar replacement.

Cherry-Almond Thumbprint Cookies
Makes approximately 24

A tasty, naturally gluten-free almond flour dough serves as a great base for this thumbprint cookie. Fill the indentation with a diabetic-friendly cherry jam as we did, or choose another favorite flavor or two.

½ cup unsalted butter, softened
2 cups bleached almond flour, plus additional for
    dipping measuring spoon
⅓ cup granulated sugar substitute*
1 teaspoon vanilla extract
½ teaspoon kosher salt
½ teaspoon fresh lemon zest
6 teaspoons spreadable cherry all-fruit jam

• Preheat oven to 350°. Line 2 rimmed baking sheets with parchment paper.
• In a large bowl, beat together butter, almond flour, sugar substitute, vanilla extract, salt, and lemon zest with a mixer at medium speed until creamy, 2 to 3 minutes, stopping to scrape down sides of bowl as necessary.
• Using a levered 2-teaspoon scoop, portion approximately 24 mounds of dough 2 inches apart onto prepared baking sheets. Press a rounded ½-teaspoon measuring spoon dipped in additional almond flour firmly into centers of dough balls to make an indentation.
• Bake until edges of cookies are light golden brown and set, 10 to 12 minutes.
• Place jam in a microwave-safe bowl. Microwave on high in 15-second intervals, stirring between each interval, until smooth and almost pourable. While cookies are still warm, spoon approximately ¼ teaspoon jam into each cookie. Let cool completely on wire racks. Store in a single layer in airtight containers and serve within 3 days.

*We used Swerve Granular sugar replacement.

Pomegranate-Chocolate Tartlets
Makes 15

Especially impressive when presented on a tiered stand, mini phyllo dough shells piped with a slightly sweet chocolate mousse, imbued with the tart flavor of pomegranate juice, are unbelievably simple to make.

½ cup pure pomegranate juice
¼ cup granulated sugar substitute*
2 ounces unsweetened chocolate, chopped
½ cup heavy whipping cream, divided
1 (1.9-ounce) box frozen mini phyllo shells, thawed
Garnish: fresh mint and pomegranate arils

• In a medium saucepan, heat together juice and sugar substitute over medium heat until boiling. Continue to cook mixture until reduced to approximately 2 to 3 tablespoons. Remove from heat.
• Whisk chocolate into hot juice until melted. Stir in 2 tablespoons cream until mixture is smooth and creamy.
• In a medium bowl, beat remaining ¼ cup plus 2 tablespoons cream with a mixer at high speed until soft peaks form. Fold whipped cream into chocolate mixture until combined. Transfer mixture to a piping bag fitted with a ½-inch French star tip (Ateco #866). Pipe mixture into phyllo shells. Serve immediately, or refrigerate for up to 2 hours.
• Just before serving, garnish with mint and pomegranate arils, if desired.

VISIONS OF
Snowmen

The
MENU

SCONE
White Chocolate–Peppermint Scones
with Peppermint Cream
Belgian Chocolate Rooibos

SAVORIES
Cucumber-Turmeric Tea Sandwiches
Chicken Salad Tea Sandwiches
Broccoli-Havarti Quiches
Chestnut Black Tea

SWEETS
Snowman Macarons
Gingerbread Bars with
White Chocolate Mousse
Red Velvet Cake Truffles
Frosty Plum Spice Tea

Tea Pairings by The Tea Shoppe
304-413-0890 | theteashoppewv.com

*This whimsical tea set tips
its hat to the beloved holiday
character Frosty the Snowman
making it a delightful wintry
motif for tea party guests of
all ages.*

White Chocolate–Peppermint Scones
Makes 12

Crushed peppermint candies are right at home with white chocolate chips in these teatime treats that are perfect for a Christmas afternoon tea. For a festive presentation, garnish the platter with mint and sugared raspberries.

¾ cup all-purpose flour
½ cup bread flour
¼ cup granulated sugar
1 tablespoon baking powder
¼ teaspoon fine sea salt
⅛ teaspoon vanilla bean paste
6 tablespoons cold unsalted butter, cubed
½ cup white chocolate chips
1 tablespoon finely crushed peppermint candies
½ cup plus 2 tablespoons half-and-half, divided
1 large egg

• Preheat oven to 375°. Line a rimmed baking sheet with parchment paper.
• In a large bowl, whisk together all-purpose flour, bread flour, sugar, baking powder, salt, and vanilla bean paste. Using a pastry blender or 2 forks, cut butter into flour mixture until it resembles coarse crumbs. Add chocolate chips and peppermint candies, stirring until combined. Add ½ cup half-and-half, stirring until mixture is evenly moist. Working gently, bring mixture together with hands until a dough forms. (If dough seems dry, add more half-and-half, 1 tablespoon at a time.)
• Turn out dough onto a lightly floured surface, and knead gently until smooth by patting dough and folding it in half 4 to 5 times. Using a rolling pin, roll out dough to a ½-inch thickness. Using a 2-inch fluted round cutter dipped in flour, cut 12 scones from dough without twisting cutter, rerolling scraps as necessary.
• In a small bowl, whisk together egg and remaining 2 tablespoons half-and-half to make an egg wash. Brush tops of scones with egg wash. Freeze scones for 10 minutes.
• Bake until edges of scones are golden brown and a wooden pick inserted in centers comes out clean, approximately 16 minutes. Let cool slightly on a wire rack. Serve warm.

RECOMMENDED CONDIMENT:
Peppermint Cream (recipe follows)

Peppermint Cream
Makes approximately 2 cups

This tasty candy-laced spread is a dessert in and of itself.

1 cup cold heavy whipping cream
1 teaspoon confectioners' sugar
1 teaspoon vanilla extract
1 tablespoon finely crushed peppermint candies, divided

• In a medium bowl, beat together cream, confectioners' sugar, and vanilla extract with a mixer at high speed until thickened and creamy. Cover, and refrigerate until needed, up to 2 hours.
• Just before serving, transfer cream to a serving bowl. Fold 1½ teaspoons peppermint candies into cream, and sprinkle remaining 1½ teaspoons peppermint candies onto cream.

Cucumber-Turmeric Tea Sandwiches

Makes 12

Vibrant turmeric, lime juice, and fresh mint combine to create an unexpectedly refreshing mascarpone cheese filling for a light tea sandwich that contrasts wonderfully with a selection of heartier winter fare.

2 English cucumbers, peeled
½ cup mascarpone cheese
2 teaspoons fresh lime juice
¾ teaspoon finely chopped fresh mint
½ teaspoon kosher salt
¼ teaspoon ground turmeric
¼ teaspoon Dijon mustard
⅛ teaspoon ground black pepper
6 very thin slices white bread, frozen

• Using a sharp knife, cut each cucumber into 3-inch-long pieces. Using a mandoline on setting 3, slice cucumbers lengthwise. Let cucumber slices rest between layers of paper towels before assembling sandwiches.
• In a small bowl, whisk together mascarpone cheese, lime juice, mint, salt, turmeric, mustard, and pepper. Transfer mixture to an airtight container, and refrigerate until needed, up to 4 days.
• Spread 2 tablespoons mascarpone mixture onto 3 frozen bread slices. Arrange 2 layers of cucumber slices over mascarpone mixture. Cover with remaining bread slices to create 3 sandwiches.
• Using a serrated bread knife in a gentle sawing motion, trim and discard crusts from sandwiches. Cut each sandwich into 4 (3x1-inch) rectangles. Serve immediately, or cover with damp paper towels, place in an airtight container, refrigerate, and serve within an hour.

Chicken Salad Tea Sandwiches

Makes 12

Chicken salad is a versatile filling that can be enhanced with a myriad of ingredients. The inclusion of fresh sage and shallot add a delightful herbaceous touch to these classic teatime sandwiches.

1 tablespoon unsalted butter
¼ teaspoon minced garlic
1 tablespoon finely diced shallot
½ teaspoon finely chopped fresh sage
¼ cup mayonnaise
⅛ teaspoon fine sea salt
1 dash ground black pepper
1½ cups shredded rotisserie chicken
¼ cup roughly chopped toasted pecans
6 very thin slices wheat bread, frozen
3 leaves green leaf lettuce

• In a small sauté pan, melt butter over medium heat. Add garlic; cook until fragrant, 2 to 3 minutes. Add shallot and sage; cook for 2 minutes. Transfer garlic mixture to a heatproof bowl. Let cool completely.
• In a large bowl, whisk together mayonnaise, salt, and pepper. Add garlic mixture, stirring until combined. Add chicken and pecans, stirring until incorporated. Transfer chicken salad to an airtight container and refrigerate until needed, up to 3 days.
• Spread a thick layer of chicken salad onto 3 frozen bread slices. Top chicken salad layer with a piece of lettuce. Cover with remaining bread slices to create 3 sandwiches.
• Using a serrated bread knife in a gentle sawing motion, trim and discard crusts from sandwiches. Cut each sandwich into 4 (3x1-inch) rectangles. Serve immediately, or cover with damp paper towels, place in an airtight container, refrigerate, and serve within 2 hours.

Broccoli-Havarti Quiches

Makes 24

Delicious quiches—enhanced by rich Havarti cheese, broccoli florets, red bell pepper, and green onions—incorporate a beautiful combination of colors to create a fabulous and festive savory.

1 (14.1-ounce) package refrigerated piecrust dough
  (2 sheets)
4 large eggs, divided
¾ cup half-and-half
½ teaspoon garlic powder
⅛ teaspoon fine sea salt
⅛ teaspoon ground black pepper
1 cup finely chopped broccoli florets
¾ cup finely shredded Havarti cheese
⅓ cup finely diced red bell pepper
¼ cup shredded Italian cheese blend
3 tablespoons minced green onion

• Preheat oven to 400°. Spray a 24-well mini muffin pan with cooking spray.

• Unroll both sheets of piecrust dough onto a lightly floured surface. Using a 2-inch round cutter, cut 12 circles from each sheet of dough. Transfer circles to prepared wells, pressing into bottom and up sides. Using a sharp paring knife, trim excess dough. Gently prick bottoms of crusts with a fork. Freeze for 10 minutes.

• In a small bowl, lightly whisk 1 egg. Brush egg onto dough. Top each well with a small piece of parchment paper or a mini cupcake paper liner, letting ends extend over edges of wells. Add pie weights or dried beans.

• Bake until crusts are light golden brown, approximately 10 minutes. Let cool on a wire rack for 10 minutes. Carefully remove paper and weights. Reduce oven temperature to 350°.

• In a large bowl, whisk together half-and-half, garlic powder, salt, pepper, and remaining 3 eggs. Add broccoli, Havarti cheese, bell pepper, Italian cheese, and green onion, stirring until combined. Spoon 1 table-spoon filling into each prepared well of muffin pan.

• Bake until filling is set, 15 to 20 minutes. Let cool in pan for 2 minutes. Carefully remove from pan, and serve warm.

MAKE-AHEAD TIP: Quiches can be baked a day in advance, placed in an airtight container, and refrigerated until needed. Reheat on a rimmed baking sheet in a 350° oven for 3 to 5 minutes.

Snowman Macarons

Makes approximately 36

Children will marvel at these cute and scrumptious snowman-shaped macarons, filled with a decadent Coconut Filling.

3 large egg whites
¼ teaspoon vanilla bean paste
⅛ teaspoon fine sea salt
2 tablespoons granulated sugar
1½ cups confectioners' sugar
1¼ cups finely ground almond flour
Pearl shimmering food color spray
Black and orange edible food markers
Coconut Filling (recipe follows)

• Place egg whites in a medium bowl, and let stand at room temperature, uncovered, for exactly 3 hours. (Aging the egg whites in this manner is essential to creating perfect macarons.)
• Line 3 rimmed baking sheets with parchment paper. Using a pencil, draw 24 snowman shapes 2 inches apart onto each parchment paper sheet; turn parchment over. (Snowmen shapes should be approximately 1¼ inches wide at the base and ¾ inch wide at the top, and approximately 2½ inches tall.)
• In the bowl of a stand mixer fitted with the whisk attachment, beat together egg whites, vanilla bean paste, and salt at medium-high speed until frothy. Gradually beat in granulated sugar. Increase mixer speed to high, and beat until stiff peaks form, 3 to 5 minutes. (Egg whites will be thick, creamy, and shiny.)
• In a large bowl, sift together confectioners' sugar and almond flour three times. Gently fold confectioners' sugar mixture into egg white mixture in three additions until batter falls off a spatula in thick ribbons. Let batter stand for 15 minutes.
• Transfer batter to a piping bag fitted with a small round tip (Ateco #802). Beginning at top circle of each snowman shape, pipe batter onto drawn snowman circles on prepared baking sheets. Tap baking sheets vigorously on counter 5 to 7 times to release air bubbles. Let stand at room temperature for 45 minutes to 1 hour before baking to help develop the macaron's crisp exterior when baked. Macarons should feel dry to the touch and not stick to the finger.
• Preheat oven to 275°.
• Bake until macaron shells are firm to the touch, 25 to 30 minutes. Let cool completely on baking sheets.
• Spray tops of macaron shells with food color spray. Let dry. Using edible food markers, draw snowman faces and buttons on half of macaron shells. Store macaron shells, with layers separated by parchment paper, in an airtight container, and refrigerate until ready to fill.
• Place Coconut Filling in a piping bag fitted with a medium round tip (Ateco #805). Pipe Coconut Filling onto flat side of blank macaron shells. Place macaron shells with snowman faces, flat side down, on top of filling.

MAKE-AHEAD TIP: Macaron shells can be frozen for up to 3 months in an airtight container with layers separated by parchment paper. Let thaw for 10 minutes before filling.

Coconut Filling

Makes approximately 2 cups

Toasting the flaked coconut creates a hint of nuttiness that adds a rich depth of flavor to this sweet filling.

1 cup unsalted butter, softened
¼ cup coconut milk
¼ teaspoon kosher salt
2 cups confectioners' sugar
½ cup toasted unsweetened flaked coconut, cooled

• In a large bowl, beat butter with a mixer at medium-low speed until creamy, 3 to 4 minutes, stopping to scrape down sides of bowl. Add coconut milk and salt, beating until combined. Add confectioners' sugar and coconut, beating until well combined. Use immediately.

"When a snowflake falls, a snowman somewhere is blowing you a kiss."
—AUTHOR UNKNOWN

Gingerbread Bars
Makes 48

While traditionally presented as a Christmas cookie, the classic ingredients for gingerbread are just as wonderful when served as bars and topped with a lemony White Chocolate Mousse.

6 tablespoons unsalted butter, softened
¾ cup plus 3 tablespoons firmly packed light brown sugar
1 large egg, lightly beaten
¼ cup blackstrap molasses
1 teaspoon vanilla extract
1½ cups all-purpose flour
1¼ teaspoons ground ginger
½ teaspoon fine sea salt
½ teaspoon baking powder
½ teaspoon ground cinnamon
¼ teaspoon ground allspice
¼ teaspoon ground nutmeg
⅛ teaspoon ground cloves
¼ cup whole milk
¼ cup sour cream
White Chocolate Mousse (recipe follows)

• Preheat oven to 350°. Spray a 13x9-inch baking pan with baking spray with flour. Line pan with parchment paper, letting excess extend over sides of pan.

• In a large bowl, beat together butter and brown sugar with a mixer at medium speed until fluffy, 2 to 3 minutes, stopping to scrape down sides of bowl. Beat in egg. Add molasses and vanilla extract, beating until incorporated.

• In a medium bowl, whisk together flour, ginger, salt, baking powder, cinnamon, allspice, nutmeg, and cloves. With mixer at low speed, gradually add flour mixture to butter mixture alternately with milk, beginning and ending with flour mixture, beating just until combined after each addition. Add sour cream, beating until combined. Using an offset spatula, spread batter into prepared pan.

• Bake until a wooden pick inserted in center comes out clean, approximately 25 minutes. Let cool completely in pan on a wire rack.

• Top with White Chocolate Mousse and refrigerate for 5 minutes. Using an offset spatula, create soft diagonal lines on chilled mousse. (Mousse should be slightly set and hold a shape when doing this. If shape doesn't form, refrigerate for another 5 minutes.) Refrigerate for at least 1 hour.

• Run a sharp knife along edges of pan. Using excess parchment as handles, lift gingerbread from pan, and cut into 48 (1½-inch) bars. Store in a single layer in an airtight container, refrigerate, and serve within 2 days.

White Chocolate Mousse
Makes approximately 1½ cups

With white chocolate morsels and vanilla bean paste contributing sweetness and lemon juice imparting ideal tang, this rich mousse will soon be a favorite.

1 cup white chocolate morsels
1 cup heavy whipping cream, divided
⅛ teaspoon vanilla bean paste
¼ cup confectioners' sugar
1 tablespoon fresh lemon juice

• Place white chocolate in a large heatproof bowl.

• In a small saucepan, heat ½ cup cream over medium heat, stirring frequently, just until bubbles form around edges of pan. (Do not boil.) Remove from heat. Pour hot cream over white chocolate; whisk until chocolate melts and is smooth.

• In a large bowl, beat together confectioners' sugar, lemon juice, vanilla bean paste, and remaining ½ cup cream with a mixer at medium-high speed until soft peaks form. Fold whipped cream into white chocolate mixture. Use immediately.

Red Velvet Cake Truffles

Makes 96

Dreamy Red Velvet Cake Truffles are a decadent and delicious take on a classic dessert that is perfect to serve for a festive afternoon tea.

1 cup unsalted butter, softened and divided
1½ cups granulated sugar
3 large eggs, room temperature
½ cup sour cream, room temperature
1 tablespoon red liquid food coloring
1½ teaspoons vanilla extract, divided
1¾ cups all-purpose flour
⅓ cup unsweetened cocoa powder
¾ teaspoon kosher salt, divided
½ teaspoon baking soda
¾ cup whole buttermilk, room temperature
¾ cup cream cheese, softened
2 cups confectioners' sugar
2 (11-ounce) bags white chocolate chips, divided
Garnish: melted white chocolate

• Preheat oven to 350°. Spray a 3-inch-deep 9-inch round cake pan* with baking spray with flour. Line bottom of pan with parchment paper.
• In a large bowl, beat together ¾ cup butter and granulated sugar with a mixer at medium speed until fluffy, 3 to 4 minutes, stopping to scrape down sides of bowl. Add eggs, one at a time, beating well after each addition. Add sour cream, food coloring, and 1 teaspoon vanilla extract, beating until combined.
• In a medium bowl, whisk together flour, cocoa powder, ½ teaspoon salt, and baking soda. With mixer at low speed, gradually add flour mixture to butter mixture alternately with buttermilk, beginning and ending with flour mixture, beating until combined after each addition. Pour batter into prepared pan. Using an offset spatula, smooth top of batter.
• Bake until a wooden pick inserted in center comes out clean, approximately 40 minutes. Let cool in pan for 15 minutes. Remove from pan and let cool completely on a wire rack.
• In a large bowl, break up cooled cake into crumbs.
• In another large bowl, beat together cream cheese and remaining ¼ cup butter with a mixer at medium speed until creamy, 3 to 4 minutes, stopping to scrape down sides of bowl. Reduce mixer speed to low. Add confectioners' sugar, ½ cup at a time, beating well after each addition. Add remaining ½ teaspoon vanilla extract and remaining ¼ teaspoon salt, beating until combined. Add cake crumbs, beating until well combined. Transfer mixture to an airtight container, and refrigerate for 6 to 8 hours, or overnight.
• Line 3 rimmed baking sheets with parchment paper. Using a levered 2-teaspoon scoop, portion cake mixture into 96 truffles, leaving one side flat.
• In a medium heatproof bowl, microwave 1 cup white chocolate on high in 30-second intervals, stirring between each, until melted and smooth. Using a dipping fork, dip truffles into melted white chocolate, and place on prepared baking sheets. Working with 5 to 6 truffles at a time, let chocolate set, approximately 3 minutes. (Carefully pick up truffles and move to a clean area on parchment paper to prevent excess chocolate from sticking and creating "feet" underneath the truffle.) Repeat with remaining truffles, heating remaining chocolate as needed**.
• Garnish tops with a drizzle of melted white chocolate, if desired. When set, store truffles in a single layer in an airtight container, and refrigerate until needed, up to 4 days.

*If a cake pan this size is not available, a springform pan of the same size can be used.
**Working with 1 cup of chocolate at a time prevents all of the chocolate from turning red with cake crumbs, allowing the truffles to have a clean, white chocolate finish.

A COZY
Christmas

The
MENU

SCONE
Stollen Scones

Orange & Spice Black Tea

SAVORIES
Holiday Crab Salad Tea Sandwiches

Portobello–Cream Cheese
Tea Sandwiches

Beef Tenderloin Tea Sandwiches

Larkin's Special Blend

SWEETS
Cinnamon-Spice Red Velvet
Crinkle Cookies

Double Chocolate & Peppermint
Cream Cheese Fudge

Raspberry Meringue Bars

Egg Nog Black Tea

Tea Pairings by The Larkin Tea Company
304-707-0142 | larkintea.com

*Invite your loved ones to
congregate by a crackling fire
for a relaxed, heartwarming
affair befitting an intimate
Yuletide celebration.*

Stollen Scones

Makes 13

A classic British teatime treat combines beautifully with a traditional German Christmas bread in these delectable Stollen Scones. Sweet and tart dried fruit, a warming blend of spices, and rum give this scone plenty of festive flavor.

¼ cup chopped raisins
¼ cup chopped dried apricots
¼ cup chopped dried black Mission figs
3 tablespoons rum
3 cups all-purpose flour
¼ cup granulated sugar
4 teaspoons baking powder
¾ teaspoon ground mace
½ teaspoon fine sea salt
½ teaspoon ground nutmeg
½ teaspoon ground cardamom
½ cup cold unsalted butter, cubed
1 cup plus 3 tablespoons cold heavy whipping cream, divided
½ teaspoon pure vanilla extract
2 tablespoons sanding sugar

• In a medium bowl, stir together raisins, apricots, figs, and rum until combined. Cover and let sit at room temperature for 2 hours.
• Preheat oven to 375°. Line a rimmed baking sheet with parchment paper.
• In a large bowl, whisk together flour, granulated sugar, baking powder, mace, salt, nutmeg, and cardamom. Using a pastry blender or 2 forks, cut butter into flour mixture until it resembles coarse crumbs.
• In a small bowl, stir together 1 cup plus 2 tablespoons cream and vanilla extract. Add to flour mixture, stirring with a fork just until a dough begins to form. Working gently, bring mixture together with hands until a dough forms.
• Turn out dough onto a lightly floured surface and knead gently until smooth by patting dough and folding it in half 4 to 5 times. Using a rolling pin, roll out dough to a ½-inch thickness. Scatter half of dried fruit mixture over half of dough. Fold other half of dough over fruit mixture to enclose it. Lightly roll out dough again to a ¾-inch thickness. Repeat scattering, folding, and rolling process with remaining half of dried fruit mixture. Using a 2¼-inch round cutter dipped in flour, cut 13 scones from dough without twisting cutter, rerolling scraps once. Place scones 2 inches apart on prepared baking sheet.

• Brush tops of scones with remaining 1 tablespoon cream, and sprinkle with sanding sugar.
• Bake until scones are golden brown, and a wooden pick inserted in centers comes out clean, 20 to 25 minutes. Let cool on baking sheet for 5 minutes. Serve warm or at room temperature.

RECOMMENDED CONDIMENTS:
Clotted cream
Fig jam

Holiday Crab Salad Tea Sandwiches

Makes 16

Pumpernickel bread and a generous sprinkling of poultry seasoning impart a wonderfully complex combination of flavors to classic crab salad. Garnish with fresh sage to make these tea sandwiches extra festive.

1 (8-ounce) container lump crabmeat, picked through and chopped
½ cup mayonnaise
¼ cup finely chopped celery
1 teaspoon spicy brown mustard
½ teaspoon poultry seasoning
½ teaspoon kosher salt
½ teaspoon ground black pepper
8 thin slices pumpernickel bread
Garnish: fresh sage leaves

• In a medium bowl, gently stir together crab, mayonnaise, celery, mustard, poultry seasoning, salt, and pepper until combined.
• Spread crab salad onto 4 bread slices. Top each with a remaining bread slice to make 4 whole sandwiches.
• Using a serrated bread knife in a gentle sawing motion, trim and discard crusts from sandwiches. Cut each sand-wich into 4 finger sandwiches. Serve immediately, or cover with damp paper towels, place in a covered container, refrigerate, and serve within a few hours.
• Garnish with sage leaves, if desired.

Portobello–Cream Cheese Tea Sandwiches

Makes 12

Earthy portobello mushrooms and fresh oregano are cooked together with red onion before combining with cream cheese and Parmesan cheese in this tasty tea sandwich spread. For a delightfully eye-catching presentation, serve on marble rye bread.

2 tablespoons olive oil
2 cups finely chopped baby portobello mushrooms
1 cup finely chopped red onion
2 tablespoons chopped fresh oregano
1 teaspoon fine sea salt
½ teaspoon ground black pepper
¼ teaspoon garlic powder

1 (8-ounce) package cream cheese, softened
1 cup grated Parmesan cheese
2 tablespoons mayonnaise
8 slices marble rye bead

• In a large skillet over medium-high heat, heat oil. Add mushrooms and onions; cook until tender and browned, 10 to 15 minutes. Reduce heat to medium. Stir in oregano, salt, pepper, and garlic powder, cooking for 1 minute more. Reduce heat to low. Stir in cream cheese, Parmesan cheese, and mayonnaise. Remove from heat and let mushroom mixture cool slightly.
• Spread mushroom mixture onto 4 bread slices. Top each with a remaining bread slice to make 4 whole sandwiches.
• Using a serrated bread knife in a gentle sawing motion, trim and discard crusts from sandwiches to create squares. Cut each sandwich diagonally into 4 equal triangles. Serve immediately, or cover with damp paper towels, place in a covered container, refrigerate, and serve within a few hours.

Beef Tenderloin Tea Sandwiches

Makes 12

Strips of beef tenderloin and a delectable spread consisting of mayonnaise, horseradish, mustard, and Worcestershire sauce, create a hearty and satisfying savory perfect for a cozy afternoon.

1 tablespoon old-style mustard
1 tablespoon olive oil
1 tablespoon chopped fresh rosemary
1 teaspoon garlic powder
1 teaspoon onion powder
½ teaspoon kosher salt
½ teaspoon ground black pepper
2 tablespoons canola oil
1 (8-ounce, approximately 2-inch thick) beef tenderloin steak
½ cup mayonnaise
2 tablespoons prepared horseradish
2 tablespoons sour cream
1 teaspoon Worcestershire sauce
1 teaspoon Dijon mustard
1 teaspoon granulated sugar
1 cup arugula
12 dinner rolls, prepared according to package instructions*

- Preheat oven to 350°.
- In a small bowl, stir together old-style mustard, olive oil, rosemary, garlic powder, onion powder, salt, and pepper until combined.
- In a 10-inch cast-iron skillet over medium-high heat, heat canola oil until shimmering. Sear beef in skillet, approximately 2 minutes per side. Remove from heat and rub rosemary mixture liberally over meat. Return meat to skillet, and place skillet in oven until a food thermometer inserted into thickest portion of meat registers 130°, 15 to 20 minutes. Place skillet on a wire rack and let cool for 30 minutes.
- Using a sharp knife, slice meat very thinly against the grain.
- Using a serrated bread knife in a gentle sawing motion, cut rolls in half horizontally.
- In a small bowl, stir together mayonnaise, horseradish, sour cream, Worcestershire sauce, Dijon mustard, and sugar. Spread 1 teaspoon mayonnaise mixture onto cut sides of each roll. On bottom halves of rolls, arrange a layer of arugula over mayonnaise. Gently fold 1 to 2 beef slices and place over arugula. Cover with top halves of rolls, mayonnaise side down. Serve immediately.

*We used Sister Schubert Parker House Rolls.

Cinnamon-Spice Red Velvet Crinkle Cookies

Makes 23

Red velvet is a beloved flavor for holiday sweets. In this recipe, we combined its rich, chocolaty taste with a warming blend of spices, including cinnamon and red pepper, in these delectable cookies.

¼ cup unsalted butter, softened
⅓ cup firmly packed light brown sugar
½ cup granulated sugar, divided
1 large egg, room temperature
1 tablespoon red liquid food coloring*
1½ teaspoons vanilla bean paste**
1 cup all-purpose flour
2½ tablespoons Dutch process cocoa powder, sifted
¾ teaspoon baking powder
¾ teaspoon ground cinnamon
¼ teaspoon fine sea salt
¼ teaspoon espresso powder
⅛ teaspoon ground red pepper
¼ cup confectioners' sugar

• Preheat oven to 350°. Line a rimmed baking sheet with parchment paper.
• In a large bowl, beat together butter, brown sugar, and ¼ cup granulated sugar with a mixer at medium speed until light and fluffy, 2 to 3 minutes, stopping to scrape down sides of bowl. Add egg, beating until well combined, scraping down sides of bowl as needed. Beat in food coloring and vanilla bean paste.
• In a medium bowl, whisk together flour, cocoa powder, baking powder, cinnamon, salt, espresso powder, and red pepper. With mixer at low speed, gradually add flour mixture to butter mixture, beating just until combined and scraping down sides of bowl.
• Place remaining ¼ cup granulated sugar in a small, shallow bowl. Place confectioners' sugar in another small, shallow bowl. Using a levered 1 tablespoon scoop, drop dough into granulated sugar, coating all sides thoroughly; shape into a ball. Roll ball in confectioners' sugar and place on prepared baking sheet. Repeat with remaining dough, spacing dough balls 1 to 1½ inches apart.
• Bake until edges are just set and cracks have formed, approximately 8 minutes. Let cool on baking sheet set on a wire rack. Store at room temperature in an airtight container for up to 3 days.

*We used McCormick Red Food Color.
**We used Heilala Vanilla Pure Vanilla Bean Paste, available at heilalavanilla.com or 646-360-1198.

Double Chocolate & Peppermint Cream Cheese Fudge

Makes 36 squares

Laced with refreshing peppermint extract and a combination of bittersweet and white chocolate, then topped with crushed candy canes, this rich fudge is sure to be a favorite for teatime or anytime a sweet treat is needed.

1 (8-ounce) package cream cheese, softened
¼ teaspoon fine sea salt
4½ cups confectioners' sugar
1 (4-ounce) bar bittersweet baking chocolate*, finely chopped
¼ teaspoon espresso powder
½ teaspoon peppermint extract
1 (4-ounce) bar white baking chocolate*, finely chopped
¾ teaspoon vanilla bean paste**
½ cup finely crushed mini candy canes

• Spray an 8-inch square baking pan with cooking spray. Line with parchment paper, letting excess extend over sides of pan. Lightly spray parchment paper.
• In a large bowl, beat together cream cheese and salt with a mixer at medium speed until smooth and creamy, approximately 1 minute, stopping to scrape down sides of bowl as needed. With mixer at medium-low speed, gradually add confectioners' sugar, beating just until combined. Increase speed to medium, and beat until smooth and well combined, approximately 2 minutes, scraping down sides of bowl as needed. Transfer half of cream cheese mixture to another large bowl.
• In a medium microwave-safe bowl, combine bittersweet chocolate and espresso powder. Microwave on high in 10-second intervals, stirring between each, until melted and smooth. Stir in peppermint extract.
• Fold bittersweet chocolate mixture into half of cream cheese mixture until well combined. Press chocolate mixture into bottom of prepared baking pan. Place a piece of plastic wrap directly on surface of mixture. Using plastic wrap, smooth chocolate mixture into an even layer. Remove and discard plastic wrap.
• In another medium microwave-safe bowl, heat white chocolate in microwave on high in 10-second intervals,

stirring between each interval, until melted and smooth. Fold white chocolate into remaining cream cheese mixture until combined. Stir in vanilla bean paste.
• Spread white chocolate mixture over bittersweet chocolate mixture in pan. Top evenly with crushed candy canes. Refrigerate until firm, at least 2 hours.
• Using excess parchment paper as handles, lift fudge from pan. Using a warm, dry knife, cut fudge into 36 squares.

We used Ghirardelli 60% Cacao Bittersweet Chocolate Baking Bar and Ghirardelli White Chocolate Baking Bar.
**We used Heilala Vanilla Pure Vanilla Bean Paste, available at heilalavanilla.com or 646-360-1198.*

Raspberry Meringue Bars
Makes 18

Raspberry preserves, vanilla bean paste, and sliced almonds impart a delicate balance of sweet and nutty flavor to chewy meringue bars.

6 tablespoons unsalted butter, softened
½ cup confectioners' sugar
½ cup all-purpose flour
⅓ cup blanched almond flour
¼ teaspoon ground ginger
⅛ teaspoon fine sea salt
¾ cup raspberry preserves
¼ teaspoon vanilla bean paste*
2 large egg whites
⅛ teaspoon cream of tartar
¼ cup granulated sugar
½ cup sliced almonds

• Preheat oven to 350°. Line a greased 8-inch square baking pan with parchment paper, letting excess extend over sides of pan.
• In a large bowl, beat together butter and confectioners' sugar at medium speed until thick and creamy, approximately 1 minute, stopping to scrape down sides of bowl.
• In a medium bowl, whisk together all-purpose flour, almond flour, ginger, and salt. With mixer at medium-low speed, gradually add flour mixture to butter mixture, beating until combined and scraping down sides of bowl as needed. Press dough evenly into bottom of prepared pan.
• Bake until edges are lightly golden, 12 to 14 minutes. Let cool on a wire rack for 15 minutes. (Crust will puff during baking and deflate while cooling.)

• In a small bowl, stir together raspberry preserves and vanilla bean paste until combined. Using an offset spatula, spread evenly over crust.
• In another large bowl, beat together egg whites and cream of tartar with a mixer fitted with a whisk attachment at medium-high speed until soft peaks form. Gradually add granulated sugar, beating until firm peaks form.
• Spread meringue mixture evenly over preserves, swirling as desired. Sprinkle with almonds.
• Bake until golden brown, 20 to 25 minutes. Let cool completely in pan on a wire rack. Using excess parchment as handles, lift from pan.
• Using a sharp knife, trim and discard edges, if desired. Cut into 18 rectangular bars. Serve immediately, or store in a single layer in an airtight container and refrigerate until ready to serve, up to a day. Serve cold or at room temperature.

We used Heilala Vanilla Pure Vanilla Bean Paste, available at heilala vanilla.com or 646-360-1198.

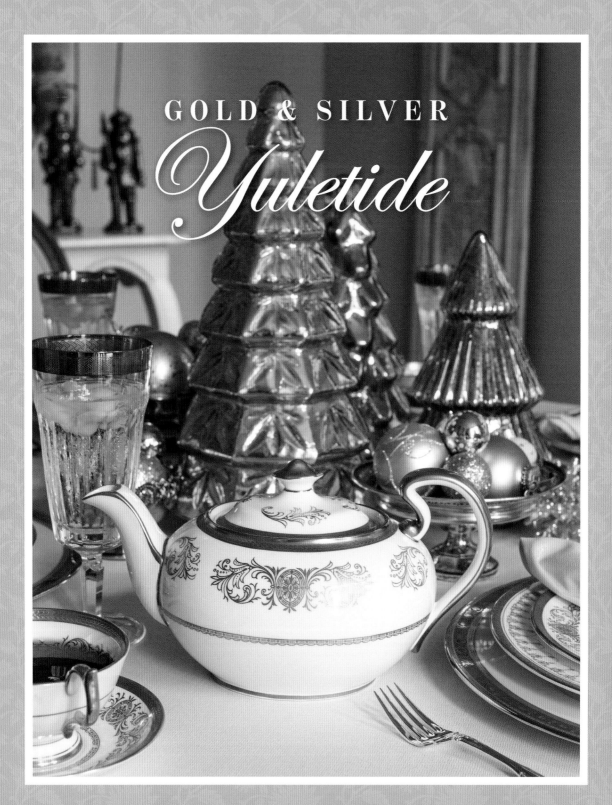

GOLD & SILVER
Yuletide

The
MENU

SCONE
Gruyère-Nutmeg Scones

Countdown to Christmas Rooibos

SAVORIES
Cucumber Canapés

Tarragon Chicken Salad
Tea Sandwiches

Smoked Salmon Tea Sandwiches with
Lemon, Caper & Dill Mayonnaise

Snow Angel Tea

SWEETS
Mulling Spice Snowball Cookies

No-Bake Maple Cheesecake Tartlets

Chocolate Truffle Bundt Cake with
Bittersweet Chocolate Ganache

Après Ski Black Tea

Tea Pairings by Tea by Two
410-838-8611 | teabytwo.com

A table bedecked in
shimmering metallics is
perfect for an intimate yet
elegant gathering for the
holiday season.

Gruyère-Nutmeg Scones

Makes approximately 16

These inventive savory scones are laced with ground nutmeg and Gruyère cheese for a nutty and rich treat perfect for a wintertime afternoon tea.

3 cups all-purpose flour
1 tablespoon granulated sugar
1 tablespoon baking powder
1¼ teaspoons ground nutmeg, divided
¾ teaspoon salt
½ cup cold unsalted butter, cubed
⅔ cup finely shredded Gruyère cheese
1 cup plus 3½ tablespoons cold heavy whipping cream, divided

• Preheat oven to 400°. Line 2 baking sheets with parchment paper.
• In a large bowl, whisk together flour, sugar, baking powder, 1 teaspoon nutmeg, and salt. Using a pastry blender or 2 forks, cut butter into flour mixture until it resembles coarse crumbs. Add cheese, stirring until combined.

• Gradually add 1 cup plus 2½ tablespoons cream to flour mixture, stirring with a fork just until a dough begins to form. Working gently, bring mixture together with hands until a dough forms. (If dough won't come together, add more cream, 1 tablespoon at a time, until it does.)
• Turn out dough onto a lightly floured surface and knead gently until smooth by patting dough and folding it in half 4 to 6 times. Using a rolling pin, roll out dough to a ¾-inch thickness. Using a 2-inch fluted round cutter dipped in flour, cut 16 scones from dough without twisitng cutter, rerolling scraps as needed. Place scones 2 inches apart on prepared baking sheets.
• Brush tops of scones with remaining 1 tablespoon cream. Lightly sprinkle with remaining ¼ teaspoon nutmeg.
• Bake until scones are lightly browned, 13 to 15 minutes. Let cool on pan for 10 minutes. Serve warm or at room temperature.

RECOMMENDED CONDIMENTS:
Clotted cream
Pear preserves

Cucumber Canapés
Makes 24

Tangy goat cheese and a fragrant blend of spices beautifully flavor the spread for this refreshing cucumber canapé, topped with crunchy yellow bell pepper. Use differently shaped cutters, like the snowflake cutter we chose, to give this tasty bite an added touch of festive flair.

24 (approximately ¼-inch-thick) slices English
    cucumber
1 (4-ounce) log goat cheese
¼ cup heavy whipping cream
2 tablespoons unsalted butter, softened
2 tablespoons mascarpone cheese, room temperature
¼ teaspoon garlic powder
¼ teaspoon onion powder
½ teaspoon kosher salt
½ teaspoon ground white pepper
½ teaspoon ground dried sage
2 tablespoons finely diced yellow bell pepper

• Using a 1¾-inch snowflake-shaped cutter, cut 24 snowflake shapes from cucumber slices, discarding scraps. Place cucumber snowflakes on paper towels.
• In the work bowl of a food processor, combine goat cheese, cream, butter, mascarpone cheese, garlic powder, onion powder, salt, pepper, and sage, processing until smooth. Transfer cheese mixture to a piping bag fitted with a medium open star tip (Wilton #4B).
• Pipe approximately 2 teaspoons cheese mixture onto centers of cucumber snowflakes. Top with yellow bell pepper. Serve immediately, or place in a single layer in a paper towel–lined covered container, refrigerate, and serve within a few hours.

Tarragon Chicken Salad Tea Sandwiches
Makes 12

The subtle licorice-like notes in fresh tarragon, along with honey and whole-grain mustard, elevate the flavor of a traditional chicken salad to a new level, especially when served in triple-stack fashion on pumpernickel and white breads.

2 cups chopped rotisserie chicken
½ cup mayonnaise
3 tablespoons chopped fresh tarragon
2 tablespoons whole-grain mustard
4 teaspoons sherry vinegar

4 teaspoons honey
1 teaspoon kosher salt
1 teaspoon ground black pepper
8 very thin slices white sandwich bread
4 slices dark pumpernickel bread

• In the work bowl of a food processor, pulse chicken until very finely chopped.
• In a medium bowl, stir together mayonnaise, tarragon, mustard, vinegar, honey, salt, and pepper until well combined. Add chicken to mayonnaise mixture, stirring until combined.
• Spread approximately 2 tablespoons chicken salad onto a white bread slice. Top with a pumpernickel bread slice and spread with 2 tablespoons chicken salad. Top with a white bread slice to make a triple-stack sandwich. Repeat with remaining bread slices and chicken salad to make a total of 4 triple-stack sandwiches.
• Using a serrated bread knife in a gentle sawing motion, trim and discard crusts from sandwiches. Cut each sandwich into 3 finger sandwiches. Serve immediately, or cover with damp paper towels, place in a covered container, refrigerate, and serve within a few hours.

Smoked Salmon Tea Sandwiches with Lemon, Caper & Dill Mayonnaise
Makes 16

Smoked salmon and a piquant mayonnaise-based spread made with fresh lemon juice, hot sauce, and capers create a flavorful tea sandwich that is sure to delight.

½ cup mayonnaise
1 tablespoon chopped fresh dill
½ tablespoon chopped capers
½ teaspoon fresh lemon zest
½ tablespoon fresh lemon juice
¼ teaspoon hot sauce
8 slices white bread
8 ounces thinly sliced smoked salmon

• In a small bowl, stir together mayonnaise, dill, capers, lemon zest, lemon juice, and hot sauce.
• Spread approximately 1 tablespoon mayonnaise mixture onto each bread slice. On mayonnaise side of 4 bread slices, place a thin layer of smoked salmon, making sure to cover entire bread slice and trimming to fit, if necessary. Top each with a remaining bread slice, mayonnaise side down, to make 4 whole sandwiches.

• Using a serrated bread knife in a gentle sawing motion, trim and discard crusts from each sandwich to create a square. Cut each sandwich diagonally into 4 equal triangles. Serve immediately, or cover with damp paper towels, place in a covered container, refrigerate, and serve within a few hours.

Mulling Spice Snowball Cookies

Makes 24

*Perfect little "snowball" tea cakes flavored with fresh
orange zest, vanilla extract, and warming spices are
dusted while warm with confectioners' sugar to brilliantly
fit into a winter white theme.*

½ cup unsalted butter, softened
¼ cup granulated sugar
¼ teaspoon fresh orange zest

¼ teaspoon vanilla extract
1 cup all-purpose flour
¾ cup very finely chopped toasted pecans
½ teaspoon ground cinnamon
½ teaspoon ground ginger
½ teaspoon ground cloves
¼ teaspoon fine sea salt
¼ teaspoon ground nutmeg
⅛ teaspoon ground black pepper
¾ cup confectioners' sugar

- Preheat oven to 325°. Line a rimmed baking sheet with parchment paper.
- In a large bowl, beat together butter, granulated sugar, and orange zest with a mixer at medium speed until fluffy, approximately 2 minutes, stopping to scrape down sides of bowl. Add vanilla extract, beating until incorporated.
- In a medium bowl, whisk together flour, pecans, cinnamon, ginger, cloves, salt, nutmeg, and pepper until combined. With mixer at low speed, gradually add flour mixture to butter mixture, beating just until combined, scraping down sides of bowl as necessary.
- Using a levered 2-teaspoon scoop, portion and shape dough into 24 (1-inch) balls. Place ¾ to 1 inch apart on prepared baking sheet.
- Bake until tops of cookies are lightly golden and bottoms are golden brown, 15 to 18 minutes. Let cool on pan for 5 minutes.
- Working in batches, toss warm cookies in confectioners' sugar until well coated. Transfer to a wire rack and let cool completely. Store in an airtight container at room temperature for up to 3 days.
- Just before serving, toss cookies in confectioners' sugar a second time until well coated.

No-Bake Maple Cheesecake Tartlets
Makes 12

These tasty no-bake petite desserts feature sweet chocolate tartlet shells and a rich filling made with cream cheese, vanilla bean paste, and maple extract. Pipe Cream Cheese Topping in a decorative manner for a pretty, extra-indulgent treat.

3 ounces cream cheese, softened
3 tablespoons granulated sugar
¾ teaspoon vanilla bean paste
½ teaspoon maple extract
⅓ cup cold heavy whipping cream
12 (2-inch) round straight-sided chocolate tartlet shells*
Cream Cheese Topping (recipe follows)
Garnish: assorted edible silver dragées

- In a medium bowl, beat cream cheese with a mixer at medium speed until smooth and creamy, approximately 30 seconds. Add sugar, and beat until well combined, approximately 1 minute more. Add vanilla paste and maple extract, beating until incorporated.
- In another medium bowl, beat cream with mixer at medium speed until thickened. Gradually increase speed to medium-high and beat until stiff peaks form.
- Using a rubber spatula, fold in one-third of whipped cream to cream cheese mixture until combined. Fold in remaining whipped cream, a half at a time, until well combined. Transfer mixture to a large piping bag that has a ½-inch hole cut in tip. Pipe cream cheese mixture evenly into tartlet shells. Using an offset spatula, smooth cream cheese mixture in tartlet shells. (Wipe edges of tartlet shells clean, if needed.) Refrigerate until set, at least 1 hour.
- Spoon Cream Cheese Topping into a piping bag fitted with a small open-star tip (Wilton #21). Pipe topping onto tartlets. Serve immediately, or place in a single layer in a covered container, refrigerate, and serve within a few hours.
- Just before serving, garnish with dragées, if desired.

Tartlet shells such as these can usually be purchased from grocery store bakeries or from Walmart.

Cream Cheese Topping
Makes approximately ¾ cup

The addition of cream cheese makes a classic whipped cream especially rich and dreamy.

1 ounce cream cheese, softened
2 tablespoons granulated sugar
⅓ cup heavy whipping cream

- In a medium bowl, beat together cream cheese and sugar with a mixer at medium speed until smooth and well combined, stopping to scrape down sides of bowl as needed. With mixer at medium-low speed, gradually add one-third of heavy cream, stopping frequently to scrape down sides of bowl. Gradually add remaining heavy cream, beating at medium speed until thickened. (Do not overbeat.) Use immediately.

*"Remember this December
that love weighs more than gold."*

—JOSEPHINE DODGE DASKAM BACON

Chocolate Truffle Bundt Cake

Makes 1 (10-cup) Bundt cake

The inclusion of espresso powder in this cake batter boosts the richness of the chocolate while ensuring that it is not overly sweet, and buttermilk adds a delightfully fluffy texture and a slight tang to this luscious Bundt cake.

1¼ cups unsalted butter, softened
2¼ cups granulated sugar
¼ cup firmly packed light brown sugar
4 large eggs, room temperature
2 teaspoons vanilla extract
1¼ cups all-purpose flour
¼ cup cake flour
⅔ cup Dutch process cocoa powder, sifted
1½ teaspoons espresso powder
¾ teaspoon baking powder
½ teaspoon salt
¾ cup whole buttermilk, room temperature
Bittersweet Chocolate Ganache (recipe follows)
Garnish: edible gold glitter and assorted gold dragées

• In a large bowl, beat together butter and sugars with a mixer at medium-low speed just until combined. Increase speed to medium, and beat until fluffy, 3 to 4 minutes, stopping to scrape down sides of bowl. Add eggs, one at a time, beating well after each addition. Add vanilla extract, beating until incorporated.
• In a medium bowl, whisk together flours, cocoa powder, espresso powder, baking powder, and salt. With mixer at low speed, gradually add flour mixture to butter mixture, alternately with buttermilk, beginning and ending with flour mixture, beating until combined and scraping down sides of bowl as needed.
• Spray a 10-cup Bundt pan* with baking spray with flour. Spoon batter into prepared Bundt pan. Tap pan on counter several times to evenly spread batter and get rid of as many air bubbles as possible.
• Place pan in a cold oven. Set oven to 325°, and bake until a wooden pick inserted near the center comes out clean, 60 to 70 minutes. Let cake cool in pan for 15 minutes. (Bottom crust may crack slightly like a brownie.) Invert cake onto a wire rack set over a parchment-lined baking sheet. Remove pan and let cake cool completely.
• Place Bittersweet Chocolate Ganache in a squeezable plastic icing bottle** fitted with a ¼-inch round piping tip (Wilton #12). Working quickly, pipe ganache into grooves of cake, letting excess drip off. Carefully transfer cake to a serving plate.
• Garnish with edible glitter and sprinkles, if desired.

We used a Nordic Ware 10-cup Heritage Bundt Pan.
**We used a 4-ounce Sweet Sugarbelle Icing Bottle with Coupler.*

Bittersweet Chocolate Ganache

Makes approximately 1⅓ cups

You'll want to spread or drizzle this decadent ganache on all of your favorite sweets.

6 ounces bittersweet chocolate, finely chopped
1 tablespoon light corn syrup
1 tablespoon unsalted butter, softened
¾ cup heavy whipping cream

• In a large heatproof bowl, combine chocolate, corn syrup, and butter.
• In a medium saucepan, bring cream to a simmer over medium heat. Pour cream over chocolate mixture. Let stand for 5 minutes. Stir until chocolate melts and mixture is smooth. Use immediately.

A VERY VEGAN
Christmas

The
MENU

SCONE
Vegan Cranberry-Pistachio Scones

Namring Upper Second Flush Darjeeling TGFOP1 Black Tea

SAVORIES
Creamy Artichoke Tea Sandwiches

Avocado–Sweet Potato Bites

Savory Rosemary–Black Pepper Shortbread

Keemun Black Dragon First Grade Black Tea

SWEETS
Gingerbread "Cheesecake" Squares

Hot Chocolate Macaroons

Apricot-Orange Cookies

Boulder Tangerine Herbal Tea

Tea Pairings by The Boulder Tea Company
303-817-7057 | boulderteaco.com

A table adorned in blue and white is a surprising, yet stunning, choice for a holiday afternoon tea full of tasty plant-based recipes.

Vegan Cranberry-Pistachio Scones
Makes approximately 12

For a vegan-friendly first course of a holiday afternoon tea, chilled coconut oil and coconut milk replace the usual dairy in these flavorful scones that are studded with red dried cranberries and green pistachios.

6 tablespoons unrefined coconut oil
2¼ cups unbleached white fine pastry flour*
2 tablespoons golden coconut sugar
1 tablespoon baking powder
½ teaspoon fine sea salt
⅓ cup chopped dried cranberries
¼ cup chopped green pistachios**
2 teaspoons fresh orange zest
1 cup plus 1 tablespoon cold coconut milk, divided
½ teaspoon vanilla extract

• Preheat oven to 400°. Line a rimmed baking sheet with parchment paper.
• Place coconut oil in a shallow bowl. Using a fork, score coconut oil deeply to create a fine grid pattern. Refrigerate until firm, 10 to 20 minutes. Using a fork or hands, quickly break coconut oil into very small pieces.
• In a large bowl, whisk together flour, sugar, baking powder, and salt. Using a pastry blender or 2 forks, cut cold coconut oil into flour mixture until it resembles coarse crumbs. (If coconut oil is too hard or too soft, it will be difficult to work with. If too hard, let sit at room temperature for a few minutes. If too soft, refrigerate for a few minutes.) Stir in cranberries, pistachios, and orange zest until combined.
• In a small bowl, whisk together 1 cup cold coconut milk and vanilla extract. Add to flour mixture, stirring until mixture is evenly moist. Working gently and quickly, bring mixture together with hands until a dough forms.
• Turn out dough onto a lightly floured surface, and knead gently by quickly patting dough and folding it in half 4 to 5 times. Using a rolling pin, roll out dough to a ¾-inch thickness. Using a 2¼-inch round cutter dipped in flour*, cut as many scones as possible from dough without twisting cutter, gently rerolling scraps as needed. Place scones 2 inches apart on prepared baking sheet. Freeze for at least 20 minutes.
• Brush tops of frozen scones with remaining 1 tablespoon coconut milk, if desired.
• Bake until edges of scones are golden brown and a wooden pick inserted in centers comes out clean, approximately 16 minutes. Serve warm.

We used Bob's Red Mill pastry flour.
**Pistachios in the shell will yield a brighter shade of green than those that can be purchased already shelled. Shell just before using.*

RECOMMENDED CONDIMENTS:
Non-dairy whipped cream
Raspberry jam

Creamy Artichoke Tea Sandwiches

Makes 12

Chopped, canned artichoke hearts mixed with vegan mayonnaise and fresh dill create a luscious, yet simple, tea sandwich filling.

1 (14-ounce) canned quartered artichoke hearts, well-drained
½ cup vegan mayonnaise
2 tablespoons finely chopped fresh dill
¼ teaspoon ground white pepper
¼ teaspoon paprika
12 slices vegan white bread*, frozen
Garnish: fresh dill sprigs

• Using a sharp knife, finely chop artichokes. Pat artichokes dry with paper towels.
• In a medium bowl, stir together artichokes, mayonnaise, dill, white pepper, and paprika until well combined. Cover and refrigerate until chilled, approximately 30 minutes.
• Spread ¼ cup artichoke mixture onto each of 6 bread slices. Top with remaining 6 bread slices to make 6 sandwiches. Using a serrated bread knife in a gentle sawing motion, trim and discard crusts from sandwiches, creating 6 equal squares. Cut squares in half diagonally, creating 12 triangles. Cover with damp paper towels and let thaw at room temperature before serving, 10 to 15 minutes, or cover with damp paper towels, place in a covered container, refrigerate, and serve within a few hours.
• Garnish with dill sprigs, if desired.

We used Dave's Killer White Bread.

> *"My idea of Christmas, whether old-fashioned or modern, is very simple: loving others."*
>
> —BOB HOPE

Avocado–Sweet Potato Bites

Makes 16

Baked sweet potato slices are a wonderful substitute for crackers or bread in these canapés topped with a radish slice and a tomato-avocado salad boasting the bright flavor of lime-pickled red onion.

2 medium sweet potatoes (uniformly shaped and
    approximately 2½ inches in diameter)
2 teaspoons olive oil, plus more for greasing foil
½ teaspoon fine sea salt, divided
⅜ teaspoon ground black pepper, divided
¼ teaspoon ground cumin
1 tablespoon finely diced red onion
2 teaspoons fresh lime juice
1 medium avocado, pitted and finely diced
2 tablespoons diced grape tomatoes
16 thin slices radish
Garnish: sliced grape tomato

• Preheat oven to 375°. Line a rimmed baking sheet with foil and lightly grease with olive oil.
• Using a sharp knife, slice sweet potatoes into 16 (¼-inch-thick) rounds. Using a 2-inch hexagon-shaped cutter, cut a shape from each sweet potato round, discarding scraps. Place sweet potato shapes on prepared baking sheet. Brush with olive oil.
• In a small bowl, whisk together ¼ teaspoon salt, ¼ teaspoon pepper, and cumin. Sprinkle over sweet potato shapes.
• Bake sweet potatoes until tender when pierced with a fork, 6 to 8 minutes. Let cool completely on baking sheet.
• In a medium bowl, stir together onion and lime juice. Let sit for 10 minutes to pickle. Stir in avocado, diced tomatoes, remaining ¼ teaspoon salt, and remaining ⅛ teaspoon pepper until just combined.
• Just before serving, place baked sweet potato shapes on a serving platter. Place a radish slice on each sweet potato shape. Divide avocado salad among radish slices.
• Garnish each with a slice of grape tomato, if desired.

Savory Rosemary–Black Pepper Shortbread

Makes 24

While typically a dessert, this shortbread is made with vegan butter and emphasizes the savory notes of rosemary and black pepper.

1 cup vegan butter*, softened
2 tablespoons golden coconut sugar
2 cups all-purpose flour
2 tablespoons cornstarch
1 tablespoon chopped fresh rosemary
1 teaspoon ground black pepper
½ teaspoon fine sea salt

• In a large bowl, beat together butter and sugar with a mixer at medium speed until creamy and well combined, approximately 2 minutes.
• In a medium bowl, whisk together flour, cornstarch, rosemary, pepper, and salt. With mixer at low speed, add flour mixture to butter mixture in 2 additions, beating until just combined after each addition.
• Turn dough out onto a piece of parchment paper. Press into a disc. Cover with a second piece of parchment paper. Using a rolling pin, roll out dough to a ¼-inch thickness between parchment paper sheets. Transfer dough with parchment paper to a rimmed baking sheet. Refrigerate until dough is firm, approximately 15 minutes.
• Preheat oven to 300°. Line another rimmed baking sheet with parchment paper.
• Using a 1¼-inch fluted round cutter dipped in flour, cut 24 rounds from dough without twisting cutter, rerolling scraps as needed. (If dough gets too soft while rerolling scraps, chill dough until firm.) Place dough rounds, evenly spaced, on prepared baking sheet.
• Bake immediately until tops look dry and bottoms are golden brown, approximately 15 minutes. Let cool completely on baking sheet. Serve at room temperature.

We used Miyoko's Creamery European Style Cultured Vegan Butter with a hint of sea salt.

Gingerbread "Cheesecake" Squares
Makes 25

These tasty no-bake bars feature a crust made with pecans and dates plus a rich, gingery filling made from soaked cashews. Maple syrup and molasses add the perfect level of sweetness.

1 cup pitted dates
1½ cups chopped pecans
1 teaspoon ground cinnamon, divided
½ teaspoon fine sea salt, divided
2 cups unsalted raw cashews, soaked in cold water
  for 4 to 10 hours
½ cup full-fat coconut milk, shaken
⅓ cup maple syrup
¼ cup coconut oil, melted and cooled
3 tablespoons unsulphured molasses
1 tablespoon vanilla extract
1 teaspoon ground ginger
Garnish: vegan whipped cream and ground cinnamon

• Spray an 8-inch square baking pan with cooking spray. Line with parchment paper, letting excess hang over edges of pan.
• In the work bowl of a food processor, pulse dates until finely chopped. Add pecans, ½ teaspoon cinnamon, and ¼ teaspoon salt. Pulse on medium-low speed until a sticky dough begins to form, with small pecan bits still visible. (Do not overprocess, or dough will become oily.) Press dough into bottom of prepared pan.
• Drain soaked cashews. Rinse with cold water.
• In the container of a blender, blend together cashews, coconut milk, maple syrup, melted coconut oil, molasses, vanilla extract, ginger, remaining ½ teaspoon cinnamon, and remaining ¼ teaspoon salt until mixture is silky smooth and creamy, 2 to 3 minutes. Taste and adjust seasonings, if desired.
• Pour filling into prepared crust. Using an offset spatula, smooth top of filling. Tap pan on counter a few times to release air bubbles. Freeze until completely firm, at least 3 hours.
• Using a hot dry knife, cut into 25 squares. Let thaw at room temperature before serving, 10 to 15 minutes.
• Garnish with vegan whipped cream and a sprinkle of cinnamon, if desired.

MAKE-AHEAD TIP: Place Gingerbread "Cheesecake" Squares in a single layer in an airtight container and refrigerate for up to 2 weeks or freeze for up to 2 months.

Hot Chocolate Macaroons
Makes approximately 20

Cocoa powder and melted dairy-free dark chocolate stirred into these coconut-laden confections remind us of the other beloved winter beverage, hot chocolate.

1¾ cups sweetened flaked coconut
¼ cup almond flour
¼ cup Dutch process cocoa powder
¼ teaspoon fine sea salt
⅓ cup pure maple syrup
2 tablespoons coconut butter*, melted
1 ounce dairy-free dark chocolate*, melted and
  slightly cooled
1 teaspoon vanilla extract
Garnish: melted dairy-free dark chocolate*

• Preheat oven to 275°. Line a rimmed baking sheet with parchment paper.
• In a large bowl, whisk together coconut, almond flour, cocoa powder, and salt.
• In a medium bowl, whisk together maple syrup, coconut butter, melted chocolate, and vanilla extract. Add syrup mixture to coconut mixture, stirring until well combined.
• Using a levered 1-tablespoon scoop, drop heaping balls of coconut mixture approximately 1 inch apart on prepared baking sheet.
• Bake for 15 minutes. Rotate pan. Bake until dry to the touch, 10 to 13 minutes more. Let cool on pan for 5 minutes. Transfer macaroons to wire racks. Let cool completely.
• Garnish cooled macaroons with melted dark chocolate, if desired. Refrigerate until chocolate sets, approximately 10 minutes.

*We used Nutiva Coconut Manna coconut butter and Hu Dark Chocolate Gems.

Apricot-Orange Cookies
Makes approximately 30

Snowflake-shaped cookies infused with orange zest and chopped dried apricots add a beautiful, wintry touch to the sweets course of a celebratory Christmas tea. For the piped decorations, just whisk together confectioners' sugar and coconut milk for a vegan alternative to traditional royal icing.

3 tablespoons cold water
1 tablespoon ground flaxseed
¾ cup coconut sugar
⅓ cup coconut oil
1 tablespoon fresh orange zest
1 teaspoon vanilla extract
2½ cups blanched almond flour
½ teaspoon baking soda
½ teaspoon ground nutmeg
¼ teaspoon fine sea salt
½ cup chopped dried apricots
¾ cup confectioners' sugar
4 teaspoons full-fat coconut milk

• In a small bowl, whisk together 3 tablespoons cold water and flaxseed. Let stand for 5 minutes.
• In a large bowl, beat together coconut sugar and coconut oil with a mixer at medium speed until well combined, 3 to 4 minutes. With mixer at low speed, add flaxseed mixture, orange zest, and vanilla extract. Increase mixer speed to medium, and beat until combined.
• In a medium bowl, whisk together almond flour, baking soda, nutmeg, and salt. With mixer at low speed, gradually add almond flour mixture to sugar mixture, beating until combined. Fold in chopped apricots. Wrap dough in plastic wrap and refrigerate for at least 1 hour.
• Preheat oven to 350°. Line 2 rimmed baking sheets with parchment paper.
• Turn out dough onto a lightly floured surface. Using a rolling pin, roll out dough to a ¼-inch thickness. Using a 2½-inch snowflake-shaped cookie cutter dipped in flour, cut out as many cookies as possible, rerolling scraps as needed. Using an offset spatula, transfer cookies to prepared baking sheets, placing them approximately 1 inch apart.
• Bake until cookies just begin to turn golden brown around the edges, approximately 10 minutes. Let cool on baking sheets for 5 minutes. Transfer cookies to wire racks. Let cool completely.
• In a small bowl, whisk together confectioners' sugar and coconut milk until smooth. Place icing mixture in a piping bag fitted with a small round tip (Wilton #1). Decorate cooled cookies with icing, as desired. Store cookies in a single layer in an airtight container at room temperature until ready to serve.

MAKE-AHEAD TIP: Dough can be made up to 2 days in advance, wrapped in plastic wrap, and refrigerated until needed.

HAPPY

Holidays

The
MENU

SCONE
Golden Raisin & Rum Scones
Christmas in a Cup Black Tea

SAVORIES
Cucumber & Pesto Christmas Trees
Smoked Salmon Wreaths
Ginger BBQ Turkey Cups
White Radiance Black Tea

SWEETS
Strawberry-Pistachio
Thumbprint Cookies
Peanut Butter Blondies
Lemony Gingerbread Cakes
Ginger Orange Caffeine-Free Infusion

Tea Pairings by Elmwood Inn Fine Teas
800-765-2139 | elmwoodinn.com

*Vivid colors and glittery
decorations create a delightful
atmosphere for sipping copious
cups of tea and savoring
whimsical fare.*

Golden Raisin & Rum Scones

Makes 12

Inspired by the iconic flavors of rum-raisin cake, these toothsome scones are cut in wedges to mimic the tree theme of the décor. However, for a more traditional look, a round cutter can be used instead.

2½ cups all-purpose flour
⅓ cup granulated sugar
1 tablespoon baking powder
1 tablespoon fresh lemon zest
½ teaspoon fine sea salt
¼ teaspoon ground nutmeg
4 tablespoons cold unsalted butter, cubed
⅓ cup golden raisins*
1 large egg
½ cup cold heavy whipping cream
¼ cup rum**
½ teaspoon vanilla extract
1 large egg white
1 teaspoon turbinado sugar

• Preheat oven to 375°. Line a rimmed baking sheet with parchment paper.
• In a large bowl, whisk together flour, granulated sugar, baking powder, lemon zest, salt, and nutmeg. Using a pastry blender or 2 forks, cut butter into flour mixture until it resembles coarse crumbs. Stir in raisins.
• In a small bowl, whisk together egg, cream, rum, and vanilla extract. Add to flour mixture, stirring until evenly moist. (Mixture will look dry and shaggy.) Working gently, bring mixture together with hands until a dough forms. (If mixture seems dry and won't come together, add more cream, 1 tablespoon at a time. Avoid adding too much extra cream, or scones will not hold their shape when baked. Dough ball should feel firm to the touch.)
• Turn dough out onto a lightly floured surface, and knead gently until smooth by patting dough and folding it in half 3 to 4 times. Divide dough into 2 equal portions. Using a rolling pin, roll dough to a little less than a ¾-inch thickness in a round circle. Pat around edges of dough circle to neaten. Repeat with remaining dough portion. Using a long sharp knife, cut each dough circle into 6 even wedges by pressing straight down. (Shape scone edges with hands, if needed, after cutting to maintain a triangular shape.) Place scones 2 inches apart on prepared baking sheet.
• Using a pastry brush, brush tops of scones with egg white. Sprinkle with turbinado sugar.
• Bake until edges of scones are golden brown and a wooden pick inserted in centers comes out clean, 18 to 20 minutes. Serve warm.

If desired, soak raisins in ¼ cup rum or in ¼ cup water and ¼ teaspoon rum extract for 6 to 8 hours. Drain well before using.
**We used Bacardi 8 rum. Rum can be replaced with ¼ cup water and ½ teaspoon rum extract.*

MAKE-AHEAD TIP: *Scones can be cut, placed on a parchment-lined rimmed baking sheet, and frozen raw. When frozen, transfer to an airtight freezer bag and keep frozen for up to 3 months. When ready to bake, brush frozen scones with egg white and sprinkle with sugar. Bake as directed. Scones may need a few extra minutes of baking time to achieve adequate browning and doneness.*

RECOMMENDED CONDIMENTS:
Clotted cream
Fig preserves

Cucumber & Pesto Christmas Trees

Makes 12

Traditional cucumber sandwiches get a festive upgrade in these tree-shaped savories that are elevated by homemade Walnut-Arugula Pesto.

12 thin slices multi-grain white bread, frozen
1 tablespoon extra-virgin olive oil
½ red bell pepper, cored and seeded
48 very thin slices English cucumber
Walnut-Arugula Pesto (recipe follows)

• Using a 4-inch-long Christmas tree–shaped cutter, cut 12 shapes from frozen bread, discarding scraps. Cover bread shapes with damp paper towels to prevent drying out and let thaw.
• Preheat oven to 350°. Line a rimmed baking sheet with parchment paper.
• Place bread shapes on prepared baking sheet. Using a pastry brush, brush shapes with olive oil.
• Bake bread shapes until light golden brown and crisp, 8 to 10 minutes, turning over during baking, if needed, for even browning. Let bread shapes cool completely on wire racks. Once cooled, store shapes in an airtight container to keep crisp, and use the same day.
• Using a ½-inch star-shaped Linzer-style cutter, cut 12 stars from red bell pepper, discarding scraps. Blot dry on paper towels before using.
• Cut cucumber slices in half. Blot dry on paper towels before using.
• Using an offset spatula, spread an even layer of Walnut-Arugula Pesto onto bread shapes. Arrange cucumber halves on top of pesto in a shingled fashion, trimming as needed to fit contours. Place bell pepper stars on top of cucumber layer. Keep cold and serve within an hour.

Walnut-Arugula Pesto

Makes 1 cup

Walnuts, arugula, parsley, Parmesan cheese, and lemon combine to produce a tasty spread for our Cucumber-Pesto Christmas Trees.

2 cups loosely packed arugula
1 cup walnut halves, toasted

½ cup freshly grated Parmesan cheese
¼ cup loosely packed flat-leaf parsley leaves
  (stems removed)
1 tablespoon fresh lemon zest
1 tablespoon fresh lemon juice
¾ teaspoon fine sea salt
⅛ teaspoon ground black pepper
⅓ cup mild extra-virgin olive oil, plus extra for topping

• In the work bowl of a food processor, pulse together arugula, walnuts, cheese, parsley, lemon zest, lemon juice, salt, and pepper. With processor running, add oil in a slow stream until mixture is fairly creamy and smooth. Add extra oil, if needed, to achieve desired consistency.
• Transfer pesto to an airtight container or jar, top pesto with a thin layer of olive oil, and place plastic wrap onto surface of pesto. Refrigerate and use within 3 days.

Smoked Salmon Wreaths

Makes 12

Charmingly whimsical in shape and classically delectable in taste, these darling wreath-like sandwiches will be the stars of your holiday tea table.

12 very thin slices white bread, frozen
1 (4-ounce) package thinly sliced smoked salmon
¼ bell pepper, cored and seeded
Creamy Horseradish Spread (recipe follows)
¼ cup very finely chopped flat-leaf parsley
1 tablespoon fresh lemon zest

• Using a 2-inch fluted round cutter, cut 24 rounds from frozen bread, discarding scraps. Using a 1-inch round fluted Linzer-type cutter, cut out and discard centers from 12 bread rounds. Cover bread rounds with damp paper towels to prevent drying out during assembly.
• Separate salmon slices and place on a cutting surface. Using the same 2-inch cutter, cut 12 rounds from salmon slices.
• Using a sharp paring knife, cut bell pepper into thin strips. Cut each strip into very small even pieces to use as "berries" on wreaths. Blot bell pepper pieces on paper towels before using.
• Spread a layer of Creamy Horseradish Spread onto all bread rounds. Top spread side of whole rounds with salmon rounds.
• Sprinkle parsley evenly over spread side of cutout bread rounds. Arrange bell pepper "berries" on top of parsley. Sprinkle with lemon zest. Place decorated bread rounds on top of salmon to create wreath sandwiches. Serve immediately, or place in a covered container, refrigerate, and serve within an hour.

MAKE-AHEAD TIP: If cutting bread a day in advance, store bread rounds in a resealable plastic bag to prevent drying out.

Creamy Horseradish Spread

Makes ¼ cup

This satisfying spread is perfectly suited for our Smoked Salmon Wreaths but would be equally divine on all sorts of tea sandwiches, especially beef.

2 tablespoons mayonnaise
1 tablespoon sour cream
1 teaspoon creamy prepared horseradish
½ teaspoon fresh lemon juice
⅛ teaspoon fine sea salt
⅛ teaspoon ground black pepper

• In a small bowl, stir together mayonnaise, sour cream, horseradish, lemon juice, salt, and pepper. Cover, refrigerate, and use within a day.

Ginger BBQ Turkey Cups

Makes 32

Petite cups, made from wonton wrappers, serve as perfect vessels for a flavorful Asian-inspired filling.

4 tablespoons olive oil, divided
32 square wonton wrappers
1 tablespoon canola oil
½ cup finely chopped red onion
⅓ cup finely chopped celery
½ tablespoon Asian chili garlic sauce
½ tablespoon finely grated fresh ginger
⅛ teaspoon fine sea salt
⅛ teaspoon ground black pepper
1 pound ground turkey meat*
½ teaspoon minced dried garlic
½ cup hoisin sauce
½ cup drained petite diced canned tomatoes
2 tablespoons fresh lime juice
Garnish: dill relish, shredded lettuce, and chopped fresh tomato

• Preheat oven to 400°. Using a pastry brush, lightly brush 32 wells of a mini muffin pan with 2 tablespoons olive oil.
• Brush one side of wonton wrappers with remaining 2 tablespoons olive oil. Press wrappers into prepared wells of muffin pan (oil-brushed sides up) forming a basket shape. (Make sure bottoms are flat so that cups will sit level after baking.)
• Bake until wrappers are crispy and edges are golden brown, 5 to 6 minutes. Remove from pan, and place on a wire rack to let cool completely. (For best texture, use the same day.)
• In a large sauté pan, heat canola oil over medium-high heat until shimmering. Add onion, celery, chili garlic sauce, ginger, salt, and pepper. Reduce heat to medium-low and cook, stirring frequently, until vegetables soften, 5 to 7 minutes. Add turkey and garlic. Increase heat to medium-high and cook, stirring to break up meat finely, until no pink remains. Add hoisin sauce, canned

tomatoes, and lime juice; bring mixture to a boil, stirring frequently. Once mixture boils, reduce heat to medium-low and cook, stirring occasionally, until mixture thickens, approximately 20 minutes.
• Just before serving, divide warm turkey filling among wonton cups.
• Garnish with dill relish, lettuce, and fresh tomatoes, if desired. Serve immediately.

*Ground turkey, which includes white and dark meat, is important for the flavor and texture of the meat filling.

MAKE-AHEAD TIP: Turkey filling can be made a day in advance, stored in a covered container, and refrigerated. Warm gently before using.

Strawberry-Pistachio Thumbprint Cookies

Makes 46

Strawberry jam placed in the center of each pistachio cookie adds marvelous taste and festive color to this fruity and nutty sweet that is best accompanied by a cup of hot tea.

1 cup unsalted butter, softened
⅔ cup granulated sugar
2 large egg yolks
½ teaspoon vanilla extract

1¾ cup all-purpose flour
½ cup finely ground unsalted roasted pistachios
¼ teaspoon fine sea salt
½ cup chopped roasted, salted pistachios
1 cup seedless strawberry jam

• Preheat oven to 350°. Line rimmed baking sheets with parchment paper.
• In a large bowl, beat together butter and sugar with a mixer at high speed until light and creamy, approximately 3 minutes. Add egg yolks and vanilla extract, beating until combined.

- In a small bowl, whisk together flour, ground pistachios, and salt. Add to butter mixture, beating until incorporated.
- Using a levered 1-tablespoon scoop, drop dough 2 inches apart onto prepared baking sheets. Roll each dough portion between palms of hands into a nicely rounded ball. Roll each ball in chopped pistachios, pressing nuts firmly into dough. Place dough balls back onto prepared baking sheets. Using the tip of the thumb or the back of a round measuring teaspoon, press an indentation into top of each dough ball.
- Bake cookies until golden brown, 13 to 15 minutes. (If indentations need reshaping, press warm cookies again with the back of a rounded measuring teaspoon.) Transfer cookies to wire racks and let cool completely. Just before serving, fill each indentation with strawberry jam.

KITCHEN TIP: Process pistachio nuts in a food processor until finely ground. (Don't over-process, or a nut butter will form.)

MAKE-AHEAD TIP: Cookies can be baked, placed in an airtight container with layers separated with wax paper, and frozen for up to 2 weeks. Let thaw completely. Fill with jam just before serving.

Peanut Butter Blondies

Makes 16

These decadent bars are crowned with a warm Milk Chocolate Ganache and chopped peanuts for the ideal balance of sweet and salty in one tempting treat.

⅓ cup unsalted butter, softened
⅓ cup natural chunky peanut butter
¾ cup firmly packed light brown sugar
¼ cup granulated sugar
2 large eggs, room temperature
¾ teaspoon vanilla extract
1 cup all-purpose flour
½ teaspoon baking powder
¼ teaspoon fine sea salt
½ cup peanut butter chips
Milk Chocolate Ganache (recipe follows)
Garnish: chopped salted cocktail peanuts, divided

- Preheat oven to 350°. Line an 8-inch square baking pan with a double layer of parchment paper with edges hanging over 2 ends of pan to use as handles. Spray lightly with cooking spray.

- In a large bowl, beat together butter, peanut butter, and sugars with a mixer at medium-high speed until combined and fluffy, approximately 2 minutes. Add eggs, one at a time, and vanilla extract, beating well after each addition.
- In a small bowl, whisk together flour, baking powder, and salt. Add to butter mixture, beating until incorporated, scraping down sides of bowl as needed. Stir in peanut butter chips. Spread batter into prepared pan, smoothing and creating a level surface.
- Bake until edges are brown, blondie is set, and a wooden pick inserted into center comes out clean, 31 to 33 minutes. Let cool completely in pan on a wire rack.
- Pour warm Milk Chocolate Ganache over cooled blondie. Using an offset spatula, spread ganache until even and smooth.
- Garnish with chopped peanuts, if desired.
- Wrap pan securely with plastic wrap and place in freezer. Freeze for a few hours or up to a week.
- Lift frozen blondie from pan using parchment handles and place on a cutting surface. Using a long sharp knife, trim away and discard rough edges. Cut blondie into 16 equal squares, rinsing knife with hot water and wiping clean between each cut. Store in a single layer in an airtight container in the refrigerator and let thaw. For best flavor, serve at room temperature.
- Just before serving, garnish with more chopped peanuts, if desired.

Milk Chocolate Ganache

Makes 1 cup

Rich and creamy, this easy-to-prepare ganache is a great topping for our Peanut Butter Blondies and is equally good on cookies, ice cream, and more.

1 cup milk chocolate chips
1 pinch fine sea salt
½ cup heavy whipping cream

- In a small heatproof bowl, combine chocolate and salt.
- In a small pan, heat cream over medium-high heat until very hot, bubbles appear around edges of pan, and cream is steaming, stirring occasionally for even heating. Pour hot cream over chocolate mixture. Let sit for 1 minute for chocolate to melt. Whisk until mixture is creamy and smooth. Use immediately.

Lemony Gingerbread Cakes

Makes 21

Laced with an assortment of spices, these petite gingerbread cakes get welcome brightness with the addition of fresh lemon zest to the batter and a lovely Lemon Glaze once baked.

2½ cups cake flour
⅓ cup granulated sugar
1 teaspoon baking soda
1 teaspoon ground ginger
¾ teaspoon ground cinnamon
¼ teaspoon fine sea salt
¼ teaspoon ground mace
¼ teaspoon ground cloves

½ cup unsalted butter, room temperature
1 large egg
1 tablespoon fresh lemon zest
½ cup honey
¼ cup unsulphured molasses
¼ cup maple syrup
¾ cup hot water
Lemon Glaze (recipe follows)
Garnish: fresh kumquats and fresh lemon zest curls

• Preheat oven to 350°. Spray 21 wells of 2 (12-well) mini fluted tube pans* with cooking spray with flour.
• In a large fine-mesh sieve set over a large mixing bowl, sift together flour, sugar, baking soda, ginger, cinnamon, salt, mace, and cloves into bowl. Whisk well to combine. In order, add butter, egg, lemon zest, honey, molasses, maple syrup, and ¾ cup hot water. Beat with a mixer at low speed for 30 seconds to combine ingredients. Scrape down sides of bowl. Beat for 2 minutes at medium speed.
• Using a levered 3-tablespoon scoop, portion batter into prepared wells of pans. Tap pans lightly on counter-top to settle batter.
• Bake just until edges of cakes are golden and a wooden pick inserted in centers comes out clean, 10 to 12 minutes. Turn cakes out immediately onto wire cooling racks and let cool completely. Trim flat side of cakes, if necessary, to level. Spoon Lemon Glaze over cooled cakes and let dry completely. Store in an airtight container at room temperature and serve within 2 days.
• Just before serving, garnish cakes with kumquats and lemon curls, if desired.

We used Wilton.

Lemon Glaze

Makes 1 cup

Three simple ingredients make this tart, yet sweet, glaze that perfectly tops our mini cakes as a nod to the lemon sauce traditionally served with gingerbread.

2 cups confectioners' sugar
2 teaspoons fresh lemon zest
¼ cup fresh lemon juice

• In a medium bowl, whisk together confectioners' sugar, lemon zest, and lemon juice until smooth. Glaze should be very thin and pour easily. (Add more lemon juice, if needed, to achieve desired consistency.) Use immediately.

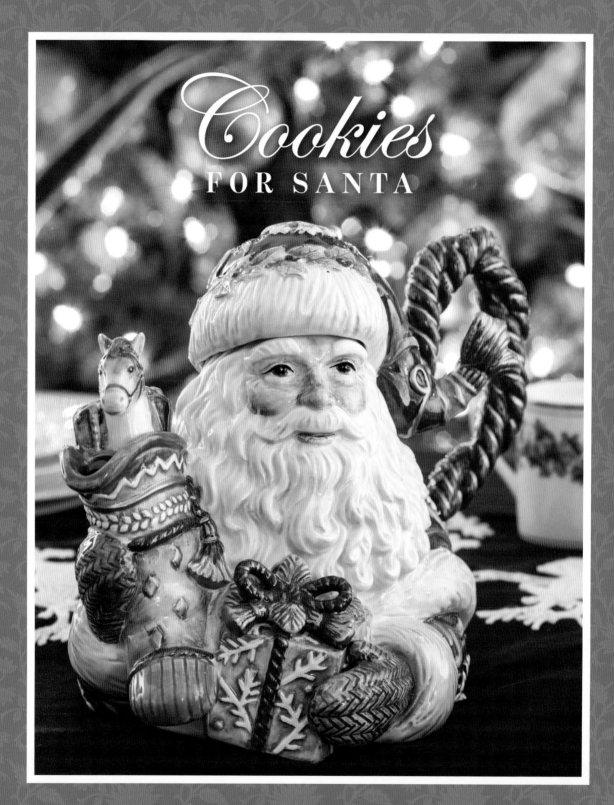

Cookies
FOR SANTA

The
MENU

SCONE
Santa Hat Scones with
Mascarpone Frosting
Berry Nice Herbal Tisane

SAVORIES
Pizza Christmas Tree Pastries

Corn Deer with
Honey-Mustard Dipping Sauce

Elf Hats
Roasted Chestnut Rooibos

SWEETS
Reindeer Shortbread
Sandwich Cookies

Candy Cane Cookies

Santa Blondies
White Chocolate Peppermint Rooibos

Tea Pairings by Simpson & Vail
800-282-8327 | svtea.com

Create a Christmas teatime wonderland that children and jolly old St. Nick will remember for years to come.

Santa Hat Scones

Makes 12

Each topped with a fresh strawberry to mimic St. Nick's iconic red hat, these charming and oh-so delicious white chocolate and coconut–laden Santa Hat Scones are sure to delight children and adults alike.

2 cups all-purpose flour
¼ cup granulated sugar
2 teaspoons baking powder
½ teaspoon fine sea salt
4 tablespoons cold salted butter, cut into pieces
⅓ cup white chocolate chips
⅓ cup sweetened flaked coconut, chopped
¾ cup plus 3 tablespoons cold heavy whipping cream, divided

½ teaspoon vanilla extract
12 fresh strawberries, stems removed
Mascarpone Frosting (recipe follows)

• Preheat oven to 350°. Line a rimmed baking sheet with parchment paper.
• In a large bowl, whisk together flour, sugar, baking powder, and salt. Using a pastry blender or 2 forks, cut butter into flour mixture until it resembles coarse crumbs. Stir in white chocolate and coconut.
• In a small bowl, whisk together ¾ cup plus 2 table-spoons cream and vanilla extract. Add to flour mixture, stirring until a dough begins to form. Working gently, bring mixture together with hands until a dough forms. (If dough seems dry, add more cream, 1 tablespoon at a time.)
• Turn out dough onto a lightly floured surface, and knead gently until smooth by patting dough and folding it in half 4 to 5 times. Using a rolling pin, roll out dough to a 1-inch thickness. Using a 2-inch round cutter dipped in flour, cut 12 scones from dough without twisting cut-ter, rerolling scraps once. Place scones 2 inches apart on prepared baking sheet. Brush tops of scones with remaining 1 tablespoon cream.
• Bake scones until edges are golden brown and a wooden pick inserted in centers comes out clean, 18 to 20 minutes. Let cool completely.
• Just before serving, place Mascarpone Frosting in a piping bag fitted with a medium open star tip (Wilton #21). Pipe a silver dollar-size circle of frosting onto tops of scones. Place a strawberry, cut side down, into center of each circle, and press down slightly. Pipe a pea-size dot of frosting onto tip of each strawberry. Serve immediately.

Mascarpone Frosting

Makes approximately 1 cup

Rich mascarpone cheese replaces traditional cream cheese in this slightly sweet frosting that is the perfect topping for a variety of baked goods.

½ cup mascarpone cheese
2 tablespoons confectioners' sugar, sifted
½ cup heavy whipping cream
¼ teaspoon vanilla extract

• In a large bowl, beat mascarpone cheese with a mixer at medium speed until thick and creamy. Gradually beat in confectioners' sugar. Beat in cream and vanilla extract. Use immediately.

Pizza Christmas Tree Pastries

Makes 12

What's not to love about individual pizza pastries in the shape of Christmas trees? Invite kids to select their favorite toppings as decoration for a more personalized take on these edible "evergreens."

½ (17.3-ounce) package frozen puff pastry, thawed
   (1 sheet)
2 tablespoons prepared pizza sauce
¼ cup cooked ground beef
3 tablespoons shredded mozzarella cheese, chopped
1½ tablespoons finely grated Parmesan cheese
12 (6-inch) wooden skewers
2 tablespoons minced fresh green onion
   (green parts only), divided
2 tablespoons chopped fresh parsley, divided
1 large egg, lightly beaten
1 tablespoon water

• Line a rimmed baking sheet with parchment paper.
• On a lightly floured surface, unfold puff pastry sheet. Using a rolling pin, roll out puff pastry to a 14x10-inch rectangle. Using a sharp knife, cut a 14x6-inch rectangle and a 14x4-inch rectangle from puff pastry.
• Using an offset spatula, spread pizza sauce onto 14x6-inch rectangle, leaving a ⅛-inch border at short ends. Sprinkle with beef, mozzarella cheese, and Parmesan cheese. Using a pastry wheel, cut dough lengthwise into 12 (½-inch-wide) strips. Working with one strip at a time, fold pastry back and forth accordion-style, creating a triangular tree shape. Insert a skewer through center of base through top of triangle to secure strip. Repeat with remaining puff pastry strips.
• Place pastry triangles 2 inches apart on prepared baking sheet. Sprinkle pastry triangles with 1 tablespoon green onion and 1 tablespoon parsley.
• From remaining 14x4-inch puff pastry rectangle, cut 12 (2x1-inch) rectangles using a paring knife and 24 stars using a 1-inch star-shaped cutter.
• In a small bowl, whisk together egg and water to make an egg wash. Brush 1 rectangle and 2 stars with egg wash, and place a small dot of egg wash at top and at center base of tree. Place rectangle, egg wash side up, under skewer at base of tree. (Long edges of rectangle should be parallel to tree base.) Fold rectangle over skewer end to form a square. Gently press square to adhere to base of tree, centering as needed. Place a star, egg wash side up, under skewer at top of tree. Cover

skewer and star with other star, egg wash side down, aligning points of stars. Press stars together gently to adhere to each other and top of tree. Lightly brush star and tree trunk with egg mixture. Repeat process with remaining rectangles, stars, and egg mixture on remaining puff pastry trees. Refrigerate for at least 30 minutes.
• Preheat oven to 350°.
• Bake pastries until edges are golden brown, 20 to 25 minutes. Let cool on baking sheet for approximately 10 minutes. Transfer puff pastry trees to a wire rack. When cool enough to handle, gently remove skewers from trees.
• Garnish pastries with remaining 1 tablespoon green onion and remaining 1 tablespoon parsley, if desired. Serve within an hour.

Corn Deer

Makes 24

A classic fair food gets a festive makeover in our adorable take on a miniature corn dog. We chose black olives and red bell pepper to make the face, but feel free to substitute your favorite veggies for a more colorful take.

24 miniature smoked sausages
½ cup all-purpose flour
½ cup fine-ground yellow cornmeal
2 teaspoons granulated sugar
2 teaspoons baking powder
¼ teaspoon fine sea salt
¼ teaspoon ground black pepper
½ cup whole milk
1 large egg
Vegetable oil, for frying
25 (6-inch) wooden skewers
Miniature pretzel twists
Mayonnaise
Finely chopped black olives
Finely chopped red bell pepper
Honey-Mustard Dipping Sauce (recipe follows)

• Preheat oven to 200°. Set a wire cooling rack on a rimmed baking sheet.
• Place sausages on paper towels to drain. Blot dry with additional paper towels, if necessary.
• In a medium bowl, whisk together flour, cornmeal, sugar, baking powder, salt, and pepper.
• In another small bowl, whisk together milk and egg. Add milk mixture to cornmeal mixture, stirring until well combined. (For easier dipping, pour batter into a short drinking glass, refilling as necessary.)
• In a large Dutch oven, pour oil to a depth of 2 inches, and heat over medium heat until a deep-fry thermometer registers 375°.
• Using scissors, cut and discard sharp points from 24 wooden skewers. Insert skewers lengthwise through center of sausages, leaving one end exposed to use as a handle.
• Working in batches, dip sausages in batter, coating evenly. Immediately and carefully place coated sausages into hot oil. Fry, turning frequently, until browned, 2 to 3 minutes. Let drain on prepared rack, and place in oven to keep warm while frying remaining sausages.
• For antlers, break up pretzel twists as evenly as possible. Using remaining skewer, make 2 small holes on each side at top of each sausage. Insert the end of a pretzel piece into each hole.
• For eyes, place 2 small dots of mayonnaise on corn dog, and gently press an olive piece into each mayonnaise dot.
• For nose, place a small dot of mayonnaise on corn dog, and gently press a bell pepper piece into each mayonnaise dot.
• Serve within an hour with Honey-Mustard Dipping Sauce.

Honey-Mustard Dipping Sauce

Makes approximately 1 cup

With just the right amount of sweetness, you'll want to dip all of your food in this creamy, three-ingredient sauce.

½ cup yellow mustard
⅓ cup sour cream
¼ cup honey

• In a medium bowl, whisk together mustard, sour cream, and honey until combined. Cover and refrigerate until ready to serve.

Elf Hats

Makes 30

Enjoy a taste of the tropics this holiday season with a whimsical treat that combines sweet and salty flavors in one perfectly balanced snack. Kids of all ages will love getting to help shape and decorate their own Elf Hats.

3 large red apples
½ (7.5-ounce) container pineapple-flavored cream cheese spread
6 (10-inch) spinach-and-herb tortilla wraps
12 deli-style ham slices
1 paper plate

• Using a vegetable peeler, peel apples vertically to create 30 (4-inch-long) peeling strips. Reserve peeling. Core apple and cut into thin slices.
• Using an offset spatula, spread an even layer of cream cheese onto tortillas. Arrange 4 ham slices over cream cheese layer on 3 tortillas. Spread a thin layer of cream cheese over ham. Place apple slices over cream cheese layer. Top with remaining 3 tortillas, cream cheese side down.
• Using scissors, cut a 4x4x3-inch triangle from paper

plate to use as a template. Position template on tortilla sandwiches so 3-inch edge of template is along rounded edge of tortillas. Using a serrated knife in a gentle sawing motion, cut 10 triangles from each tortilla sandwich.

• Place a small amount of cream cheese on the back of reserved peeling strips, and gently press onto curved end of sandwich triangles, approximately 1-inch from edge, trimming edges of peeling if needed. Serve immediately, or cover with damp paper towels, place in an airtight container, refrigerate, and serve within an hour.

Reindeer Shortbread Sandwich Cookies
Makes 14

With a decadent chocolate-hazelnut spread filling and cute icing and candy decorations, these festive shortbread sandwich cookies will charm tea guests of all ages.

½ cup unsalted butter, softened
6 tablespoons confectioners' sugar
¼ teaspoon vanilla extract
1⅓ cups all-purpose flour
⅛ teaspoon fine sea salt
⅓ cup chocolate-hazelnut spread*
Chocolate-flavored cookie icing*
Red miniature candy-coated chocolate candies*

• In a large bowl, beat together butter, confectioners' sugar, and vanilla extract with a mixer at medium-high speed until thick and creamy, 3 to 4 minutes, stopping to scrape down sides of bowl.
• In a medium bowl, whisk together flour and salt. Gradually add flour mixture to butter mixture, beating just until combined.
• Turn out dough onto a lightly floured surface and divide in half. Shape each half into a disk and wrap in plastic wrap. Refrigerate for 30 minutes.
• Preheat oven to 350°. Line 2 baking sheets with parchment paper.
• Working with one dough portion at a time, unwrap dough and place it on a lightly floured surface. Using a rolling pin, roll out dough to a ¼-inch thickness. Using a 2-inch round cutter dipped in flour, cut 28 rounds from dough without twisting cutter, and place 2 inches apart on prepared baking sheets, gently rerolling scraps as necessary. Refrigerate for 15 minutes.
• Bake cookies until edges are light golden brown, 9 to 10 minutes. Let cool on baking sheets for 2 minutes. Transfer cookies to wire racks and let cool completely.
• Spread 1½ to 2 teaspoons chocolate-hazelnut spread onto flat side of 14 cookies. Top with remaining cookies, flat side down.
• Place cookie icing in a piping bag fitted with a small round tip (Wilton #1). On one side of sandwich cookies, pipe antlers and eyes near centers of cookies. Pipe a small dot of cookie icing below eyes for nose, place a candy on top of dot, and press lightly to adhere. Let stand until frosting is dry, at least 2 hours. Store in a single layer in an airtight container at room temperature and serve within 3 days.

We used Nutella, Betty Crocker Milk Chocolate Decorating Cookie Icing, and M&Ms.

Candy Cane Cookies
Makes 22

The refreshing flavor of peppermint permeates these buttery cookies, and a sprinkle of sanding sugar gives them extra holiday shimmer and cheer.

¼ cup unsalted butter, softened
¼ cup plus 1 tablespoon granulated sugar
1 large egg yolk
¼ teaspoon peppermint extract
⅛ teaspoon vanilla extract
¾ cup all-purpose flour
⅛ teaspoon baking powder
⅛ teaspoon fine sea salt
½ teaspoon red liquid food coloring
1 tablespoon sanding sugar

• Line 2 baking sheets with parchment paper.
• In a large bowl, beat together butter and granulated sugar with a mixer at medium speed until light and fluffy, 2 to 3 minutes, stopping to scrape down sides of bowl. Add egg yolk, peppermint extract, and vanilla extract, beating well until combined.
• In a medium bowl, whisk together flour, baking powder, and salt. Gradually add flour mixture to butter mixture, beating just until combined. Divide dough in half. Beat in food coloring to one half.
• Divide plain dough in half, and shape into disks. Wrap each portion separately in plastic wrap. Repeat process with red dough. Refrigerate for 1 hour.
• Remove one portion of plain and red doughs. Divide plain dough into ½-inch balls. Using hands, roll out dough balls to 3-inch ropes. Repeat process with red dough. Place a plain dough rope and a red dough rope next to one another and gently twist together, forming a 4-inch rope. (If dough becomes too soft to work with, cover with plastic wrap and refrigerate until cold enough to use, approximately 15 minutes.) Repeat with remaining doughs. Place twisted ropes 2 inches apart on prepared baking sheets and curve an end to form a candy cane shape. Freeze for 30 minutes.
• Preheat oven to 350°.
• Sprinkle tops of cookies with sanding sugar.
• Bake until cookies are set, 8 to 10 minutes. Let cool completely on baking sheets on wire racks. Store in an airtight container at room temperature and serve within 3 days.

Santa Blondies

Makes 20 to 22

Heart-shaped blondies laden with chocolate chips are sure to satisfy a sweet tooth and please a crowd for the final course of afternoon tea, especially when artfully piped with Meringue Frosting to transform them into fun St. Nick–inspired creations.

1½ cup unsalted butter, melted and cooled slightly
1¼ cup firmly packed light brown sugar
¾ cup granulated sugar
3 large eggs
2 teaspoons vanilla extract
3 cups all-purpose flour
2 teaspoons baking powder
1½ teaspoons fine salt
Meringue Frosting (recipe follows)
Miniature semisweet chocolate chips
Red nonpareils

• Preheat oven to 350°. Line a 13x9-inch baking pan with foil, letting excess extend over sides of pan; spray foil with cooking spray.
• In a medium bowl, whisk together melted butter and sugars until smooth. Add eggs and vanilla extract, whisking until combined.
• In another medium bowl, whisk together flour, baking powder, and salt. Gradually whisk flour mixture into egg mixture just until combined. Using an offset spatula, spread batter into prepared baking pan.
• Bake until golden brown and a wooden pick inserted in center comes out clean, 20 to 25 minutes. Let cool in pan for 10 minutes. Using excess foil as handles, remove from pan, and let cool completely on a wire rack.
• Using foil to lift, place blondie on a cutting surface, and peel foil away. Using a 2¼-inch heart-shaped cutter, cut as many shapes as possible from blondie. (Make cuts as close to edges as possible to utilize space, turning cutter as necessary.) Arrange heart shapes with points at top and rounded edges at bottom.
• Place white Meringue Frosting in a piping bag fitted with a small round tip (Wilton #1). On bottom third of each blondie, pipe an outline for Santa's beard and mustache, leaving a small opening for the mouth.
• Place red Meringue Frosting in a piping bag fitted with a small round tip (Wilton #1). On top third of each blondie, pipe an outline for Santa's hat. Let stand until frosting dries, at least 1 hour.
• Using the back of a spoon or a small clean paintbrush, fill in beard with more white frosting and fill in hat with more red frosting.
• Using small dots of white frosting, glue 2 chocolate chips in place for eyes and 1 nonpareil in place for the nose on each blondie, pressing gently to adhere.
• Using white frosting, pipe a line at bottom of Santa's hat for the trim and a dot at the top for the pompom. Let stand until frosting dries, at least 1 hour. Store in a single layer an airtight container at room temperature for up to 3 days.

Meringue Frosting

Makes approximately 1½ cups

The vanilla flavor of this pipeable icing makes it an ideal topping for our Santa Blondies.

¼ cup cold water
3 tablespoons meringue powder
2 cups confectioners' sugar
Red paste food coloring
⅛ teaspoon vanilla extract

• In a medium bowl, beat together ¼ cup cold water and meringue powder with a mixer at medium speed until foamy. Gradually add confectioners' sugar, beating until smooth. (Frosting will be thick.)
• Transfer two-thirds of frosting to another medium bowl. Cover with plastic wrap directly on surface until ready to use.
• Transfer remaining one-third of frosting to a small bowl. Add desired amount of food coloring and vanilla extract, stirring until incorporated. Cover with plastic wrap directly on surface until ready to use.

"The greatest thing is not to believe in Santa Claus; it is to be Santa Claus." —PAT BOONE

TEA FOR
Christmastide

The
MENU

SCONE
Eggnog Scones with Eggnog Cream

German Gingerbread Black Tea

SAVORIES
Spiced Pineapple, Ham & Cheddar
Tea Sandwiches

Blue Cheese, Caramelized Onion &
Roast Beef Tea Sandwiches

Mustard-Glazed Salmon Crostini

Royal Empress Tea

SWEETS
Wreath Cookies

Coconut-Raspberry Squares

Dark Chocolate–Peppermint Cookies

Red Velvet–Cream Cheese Bundt Cake

White Champagne Raspberry Tea

Tea Pairings by Driftwood Tea Company
727-203-3504 | driftwoodteacompany.com

*Set the table with subtle tones
and sprigs of evergreen for
distinguished friends and
family to celebrate the joyous
holiday season.*

Eggnog Scones

Makes 14

We replaced the typical liquid used in scones with prepared eggnog and added a combination of nutmeg and cinnamon to reinforce the iconic eggnog spice in these scrumptious baked goods. Top with a generous dollop of Eggnog Cream for an added boost of festive flavor.

2 cups cake flour
2 tablespoons granulated sugar
2 teaspoons baking powder
½ teaspoon salt
¼ cup cold unsalted butter, cubed
½ cup plus 2 tablespoons cold prepared eggnog, divided
½ teaspoon ground cinnamon
½ teaspoon vanilla extract
½ teaspoon ground nutmeg, divided
1 tablespoon sanding sugar

• Preheat oven to 375°. Line a rimmed baking sheet with parchment paper.
• In a large bowl, whisk together flour, granulated sugar, baking powder, and salt. Using a pastry blender or 2 forks, cut in butter until it resembles coarse crumbs.
• In a small bowl, stir together ½ cup eggnog, cinnamon, vanilla extract, and ¼ teaspoon nutmeg. Add eggnog mixture to flour mixture, stirring until a shaggy dough begins to come together. Working gently, bring mixture together with hands until a dough forms. (If dough seems dry and won't come together, add more eggnog, 1 tablespoon at a time, until it does.)
• Turn out dough onto a lightly floured surface and knead gently until smooth by patting dough and folding it in half 4 to 5 times. Using a rolling pin, roll out dough to a ½-inch thickness. Using a 2-inch fluted round cutter dipped in flour, cut 14 scones from dough without twisting cutter, rerolling scraps as necessary. Place scones 2 inches apart on prepared baking sheet.
• Brush tops of scones with remaining 2 tablespoons eggnog.
• In a small bowl, stir together sanding sugar and remaining ¼ teaspoon nutmeg. Sprinkle mixture over tops of scones.
• Bake scones until edges are golden brown and a wooden pick inserted in centers comes out clean, approximately 15 minutes. Serve warm.

RECOMMENDED CONDIMENT:
Eggnog Cream (recipe follows)

Eggnog Cream

Makes approximately 1¼ cups

This tasty cream adds delightfully warming spice to sweet scones. If desired, add a splash of rum or rum flavoring for extra zing.

½ cup heavy whipping cream
3 tablespoons prepared eggnog
¼ teaspoon ground nutmeg
¼ teaspoon cinnamon sugar*
Garnish: ground nutmeg

• In a medium bowl, beat together cream, eggnog, nutmeg, and cinnamon sugar with a mixer at medium speed until very stiff peaks form. Transfer cream to an airtight container, refrigerate, and serve within a day.
• Garnish with nutmeg before serving, if desired.

*We used McCormick Cinnamon Sugar. Alternatively, stir together equal parts ground cinnamon and granulated sugar.

Spiced Pineapple, Ham & Cheddar Tea Sandwiches

Makes 12

This crowd-pleasing savory is simple to assemble and boasts a wonderful meld of ingredients, including sweet pineapple preserves, honey-glazed ham, and a blend of seasonal spices.

¼ cup plus 1 tablespoon pineapple preserves
½ teaspoon ground allspice
½ teaspoon ground black pepper
¼ teaspoon kosher salt
⅛ teaspoon ground red pepper
8 slices white bread, frozen
½ pound thinly sliced Cheddar cheese
¾ pound thinly sliced honey-glazed ham
Garnish: fresh thyme sprigs

• In a small bowl, stir together pineapple preserves, allspice, black pepper, salt, and red pepper until smooth.
• Spread pineapple mixture in an even layer onto frozen bread slices. Top pineapple layer of 4 bread slices with cheese. Shingle ham to fit over cheese. Cover with remaining 4 bread slices, pineapple side down.
• Using a serrated bread knife in a gentle sawing motion, trim and discard crusts from sandwiches to make 3-inch squares. Cut each sandwich into 3 (3x1-inch) rectangles. Serve immediately, or cover with damp paper towels, store in an airtight container, refrigerate, and serve within 2 hours.
• Just before serving, garnish with thyme, if desired.

Blue Cheese, Caramelized Onion & Roast Beef Tea Sandwiches

Makes 12

Sweet caramelized onion and tangy blue cheese transform deli roast beef and rye bread into an extraordinary savory offering that is sure to impress.

2 tablespoons unsalted butter
1 medium sweet onion, thinly sliced
1 tablespoon red wine vinegar
½ cup blue cheese crumbles
¼ teaspoon kosher salt
6 slices rye bread, frozen
½ pound thinly sliced roast beef
Garnish: fresh rosemary sprigs

• In a medium sauté pan, melt butter over medium-low heat. Add onion; cook, stirring occasionally, until caramelized, approximately 15 minutes. Remove from heat; transfer to a heatproof bowl. Add vinegar, stirring well. Let cool completely.
• Using a sharp knife, roughly chop caramelized onions. Add blue cheese and salt, folding until combined. Spread a layer of onion mixture onto frozen bread slices. On onion spread side of 3 bread slices, shingle roast beef to fit. Cover with remaining bread slices, spread side down.
• Using a serrated bread knife in a gentle sawing motion, trim and discard crusts from sandwiches to make 4x3-inch rectangles. Cut each sandwich into 4 (3x1-inch) rectangles. Serve immediately, or cover with damp paper towels, store in an airtight container, refrigerate, and serve within 2 hours.
• Just before serving, garnish with rosemary, if desired.

Mustard-Glazed Salmon Crostini

Makes 24

In these savory bites, baked salmon and a Dijon mustard and horseradish cream spread contrast nicely with crunchy bruschetta toasts and a sprinkling of toasted pecan pieces.

1 (4-ounce) skinless salmon fillet
1 tablespoon olive oil
1½ tablespoons Dijon mustard, divided
⅛ teaspoon kosher salt
¼ teaspoon ground black pepper, divided
¼ cup sour cream
1 tablespoon cream-style horseradish
24 bruschetta toasts
¼ cup lightly toasted pecan pieces
Garnish: celery leaves

• Preheat oven to 375°. Line a rimmed baking sheet with foil.
• Place salmon on prepared baking sheet. In a small bowl, stir together oil, ½ tablespoon mustard, salt, and ⅛ teaspoon pepper. Brush mixture onto both sides of salmon. Wrap salmon in foil of prepared baking sheet.
• Bake until an instant-read thermometer inserted in thickest portion of salmon registers 145°, 8 to 12 minutes. Unwrap foil package, and let salmon cool for 10 minutes. Using a fork, shred salmon into large pieces. Place salmon and any remaining glaze in an airtight container, refrigerate, and use within a day.

• In a small bowl, whisk together sour cream, horseradish, remaining 1 tablespoon mustard, and remaining ⅛ teaspoon pepper until smooth. Spread mixture onto toasts. Top with salmon, and sprinkle with pecans.
• Garnish with celery leaves, if desired. Serve at room temperature.

Wreath Cookies

Makes 28

Chopped pistachios and dried cranberries add a hint of festive cheer to these simple cookies.

¼ cup unsalted butter, softened
¼ cup plus 2 tablespoons confectioners' sugar
¼ teaspoon vanilla bean paste
⅛ teaspoon lemon extract
1 cup all-purpose flour
½ teaspoon fresh lemon zest, divided
⅛ teaspoon fine sea salt
1 large egg white
3 tablespoons finely chopped dried cranberries
3 tablespoons finely chopped roasted pistachios

• In a large bowl, beat together butter, confectioners' sugar, vanilla bean paste, and lemon extract with a mixer at medium speed until fluffy, 3 to 4 minutes, stopping to scrape down sides of bowl.
• In a medium bowl, whisk together flour, ¼ teaspoon lemon zest, and salt. With mixer at low speed, gradually add flour mixture to butter mixture, beating just until combined.
• Turn out dough onto a lightly floured surface, and shape into a disk. Wrap in plastic wrap and refrigerate for 30 minutes.
• Preheat oven to 350°. Line 2 baking sheets with parchment paper.
• Unwrap dough and place on a lightly floured surface. Using a rolling pin, roll out dough to a ⅛-inch thickness. Using a 1¾-inch fluted round cutter dipped in flour, cut 28 rounds from dough without twisting cutter, rerolling scraps as necessary. Using a ¾-inch round cutter dipped in flour, cut centers from rounds without twisting cutter. Using an offset spatula, transfer cookies to prepared baking sheets. Freeze for 10 minutes.
• Brush a thin layer of egg white onto cookies. Sprinkle with dried cranberries, pistachios, and remaining ¼ teaspoon lemon zest.
• Bake cookies until edges are lightly browned, 8 to 10 minutes. Let cool on pans for 5 minutes. Remove from pans and let cool completely on wire racks. Store in an airtight container at room temperature for up to 3 days.

Coconut-Raspberry Squares

Makes 48

Refreshing raspberry preserves and toasted coconut flakes wonderfully complement the rich and buttery crust in these sweet bars.

¾ cup unsalted butter, softened
1 cup firmly packed light brown sugar
⅔ cup granulated sugar
1 large egg
1 large egg yolk
2 tablespoons whole milk
1 teaspoon vanilla extract
2⅓ cups all-purpose flour
2 teaspoons cornstarch
¾ teaspoon baking soda
¾ teaspoon fine sea salt
⅔ cup seedless raspberry preserves
1 (7-ounce) bag unsweetened flaked coconut

• Preheat oven to 350°. Spray a 13x9-inch baking pan with baking spray with flour. Line pan with parchment paper, letting excess extend over sides of pan.
• In a large bowl, beat together butter and sugars with a mixer at medium speed until fluffy, 3 to 4 minutes, stopping to scrape down sides of bowl. Reduce mixer speed to medium-low. Add egg and egg yolk, one at a time, beating well after each addition. Add milk and vanilla extract, beating until combined.
• In a medium bowl, whisk together flour, cornstarch, baking soda, and salt. With mixer at low speed, gradually add flour mixture to butter mixture, beating just until combined. (Do not overmix.) Transfer dough to prepared pan. Using lightly floured hands, gently press dough into pan.
• Bake until a wooden pick inserted in center comes out clean, approximately 18 minutes. Let cool for 10 minutes. Spread with raspberry preserves, and sprinkle with coconut. Bake until coconut is toasted, approximately 5 minutes more. Let cool completely in pan.
• Run a knife along edges of pan. Using excess parchment as handles, remove from pan. Using a sharp knife, trim and discard ¼ inch from edges. Cut into 48 (1½-inch) squares. Place squares in a single layer in an airtight container, refrigerate, and serve within a day.

Dark Chocolate–Peppermint Cookies

Makes 32

Delicate cookie wafers, rich and cooling Peppermint Ganache, and an eye-catching peppermint candy garnish create a delightfully festive dessert for the Christmastime sweets course.

2 tablespoons unsalted butter, softened
½ cup confectioners' sugar
1 large egg white, room temperature
¼ teaspoon vanilla bean paste
¼ cup plus 2 tablespoons all-purpose flour
⅛ teaspoon fine sea salt
Peppermint Ganache (recipe follows)
Garnish: crushed peppermint candies

• Preheat oven to 350°. Line a rimmed baking sheet with a 16x12½-inch parchment paper sheet.
• Referring to illustration on page 132 for spacing and using a pencil and a ruler, draw 8 lines down length of parchment and 16 lines across width. Turn parchment over.
• In a large bowl, beat butter with a mixer at medium speed until creamy, stopping to scrape down sides of bowl. Gradually add confectioners' sugar, beating until well combined. Add egg white, beating until fully incorporated, stopping to scrape down sides of bowl. Add vanilla bean paste, beating until incorporated. Reduce mixer to low speed. Gradually add flour and salt, beating just until a smooth batter forms, 2 to 3 minutes. Increase mixer speed to high, and beat until batter is completely smooth, 1 to 2 minutes.
• Transfer batter to a piping bag fitted with a small round tip (Wilton #8). Referring to illustration on page 132 for placement, pipe 2½-inch lengths of batter on top of drawn horizontal lines. (There will be 16 cookies in each of the 4 columns.)
• Bake until edges of cookies are lightly browned and centers are still pale, 8 to 10 minutes. Let cool completely on pans. Store in an airtight container at room temperature and use within 3 days.
• Place Peppermint Ganache in a piping bag fitted with a small round tip (Wilton #8). Pipe Peppermint Ganache onto flat side of 32 cookies. Place remaining 32 cookies, flat side down, on top of ganache. Dip edges of cookies into crushed peppermint candies, if desired. Store in an airtight container at room temperature until ready to serve.

Peppermint Ganache

Makes approximately 1 cup

Cooling peppermint balances the slightly bitter flavor of dark chocolate for an indulgent ganache that isn't overly sweet.

1 cup 60% cacao dark chocolate chips, finely chopped
½ cup heavy whipping cream
¼ teaspoon peppermint extract

• Place chocolate in a medium heatproof bowl.
• In a small saucepan, bring cream to a simmer over medium heat, stirring occasionally. Pour hot cream over chocolate; whisk until a smooth, shiny ganache forms. Add peppermint extract, stirring until incorporated. Cover and refrigerate until chilled, approximately 30 minutes.

Red Velvet–Cream Cheese Bundt Cake

Makes 1 (10-to 12-cup) Bundt cake

The marvelous flavors of traditional red velvet cake are captured in this Bundt alternative that will certainly be the star of your Christmastime tea. Its decadent cream cheese filling is a welcome surprise that adds richness to this dreamy cake.

1 (8-ounce) package cream cheese, softened
½ cup confectioners' sugar
1 cup plus 1 tablespoon unsalted butter, softened,
   divided
1 large egg yolk
2½ teaspoons vanilla extract, divided
1¾ cups granulated sugar
3 large eggs, room temperature
1¾ cups all-purpose flour
¼ cup unsweetened cocoa powder
1¼ teaspoons baking powder
½ teaspoon fine sea salt
¾ cup whole buttermilk
1¾ teaspoons red liquid food coloring
½ teaspoon distilled white vinegar
Garnish: confectioners' sugar

• Preheat oven to 350°. Spray a 10- to 12-cup Bundt pan* with baking spray with flour.
• In a medium bowl, beat together cream cheese, confectioners' sugar, and 1 tablespoon butter with a mixer at medium speed until combined, approximately 2 minutes, stopping to scrape down sides of bowl. Beat in egg yolk and 1 teaspoon vanilla extract until smooth, approximately 2 minutes.
• In a large bowl, beat together remaining 1 cup butter and granulated sugar with a mixer at medium speed until fluffy, 3 to 4 minutes, stopping to scrape down sides of bowl. Add eggs, one at a time, beating well after each addition.
• In a medium bowl, whisk together flour, cocoa powder, baking powder, and salt. With mixer at low speed, gradually add flour mixture to butter mixture alternately with buttermilk, beginning and ending with flour mixture, beating just until combined after each addition. Stir in food coloring, remaining 1½ teaspoons vanilla extract, and vinegar.
• Spoon two-thirds of red cake batter into prepared pan. Using a small spoon, make a slight channel in batter. Fill channel with cream cheese mixture, leaving a ½-inch border around edges of pan. Using a knife, swirl together batter and cream cheese mixture, being careful not to

touch edges of pan. Spoon remaining batter over top. Swirl mixtures again with a knife, being careful not to touch edges of pan. Smooth top with a spatula.
• Bake until a wooden pick inserted near center comes out clean, 1 hour to 1 hour and 15 minutes. Let cool in pan for 10 minutes. Remove from pan and let cool completely on a wire rack.
• Garnish with confectioners' sugar, if desired.

We used Nordic Ware's 10-cup Chiffon Bundt Pan.

A FESTIVE
Brunch

The
MENU

SCONE
Cinnamon Roll Scones
Holiday Blend Tea

SAVORIES
Everything Bagel Stratas
Hash Brown Canapés
Layered Holiday Salads
American Breakfast Tea

SWEETS
Cherry Danish Christmas Tree
Cranberry-Lime Fruit Bread
with Honey Butter
Tropical Oatmeal Cookies
Figgy Pudding Tea

Tea Pairings by Simpson & Vail
800-282-8327 | svtea.com

A whimsical, celebratory tea affair with popular brunch-inspired fare will be a memorable alternative to the midmorning meal. ❧

Cinnamon Roll Scones

Makes 12

When a beloved breakfast favorite and a teatime staple combine, it creates a divinely delicious treat that is sure to start your day on a sweet note.

2 cups all-purpose flour
¼ cup granulated sugar
1 tablespoon baking powder
½ teaspoon baking soda
¼ teaspoon fine sea salt
½ cup cold unsalted butter, cubed
½ cup cold whole buttermilk
2 tablespoons unsalted butter, melted and divided
¼ cup firmly packed light brown sugar
¼ cup chopped lightly toasted pecans
¼ cup raisins
1½ tablespoons ground cinnamon
Cinnamon Roll Icing (recipe follows)

• Preheat oven to 375°. Line a rimmed baking sheet with parchment paper.
• In a large bowl, whisk together flour, granulated sugar, baking powder, baking soda, and salt. Using a pastry blender or 2 forks, cut in cold butter until it resembles coarse crumbs. Add buttermilk, stirring until a shaggy dough begins to form. Working gently, bring mixture together with hands until a dough forms. (If mixture seems dry and dough won't come together, add more buttermilk, 1 tablespoon at a time, until it does.)
• Turn out dough onto a lightly floured surface, and knead gently until smooth by patting dough and folding it in half 5 to 7 times. Using a rolling pin, roll out dough to a 13x7-inch (½-inch-thick) rectangle. Brush dough with 1 tablespoon melted butter.
• In a medium bowl, stir together brown sugar, pecans, raisins, and cinnamon until combined. Sprinkle brown sugar mixture evenly over dough. Roll up dough length-wise, keeping a tight spiral.
• Using a sharp knife, trim and discard ends of roll, creating a 12-inch log. Cut log into 12 slices (scones). Place scones ½ inch apart on prepared baking sheet. Freeze for 10 minutes.
• Brush cold scones with remaining 1 tablespoon melted butter.
• Bake scones until edges are golden brown, 14 to 16 minutes.
• Drizzle scones with Cinnamon Roll Icing. Serve warm or at room temperature.

Cinnamon Roll Icing

Makes approximately ½ cup

Arguably the best part of any cinnamon roll, this tasty icing is wonderful when drizzled on warm scones, too.

1 cup confectioners' sugar
2 tablespoons half-and-half
1 tablespoon unsalted butter, softened
½ teaspoon vanilla extract

• In a medium bowl, whisk together confectioners' sugar, half-and-half, butter, and vanilla extract until smooth. (If necessary, add more half-and-half to achieve desired consistency.) Use immediately.

Everything Bagel Stratas

Makes 6

What could be better for a Christmas morning celebration than individual stratas boasting the delightful tastes of an everything bagel? Diced capers, chopped red onion, Dijon mustard, smoked salmon, cream cheese, and everything bagel seasoning, of course, help to flavor this delectable savory.

4 ounces cream cheese, softened
¾ cup chopped red onion
1 teaspoon diced capers
1 teaspoon everything bagel seasoning
4 large whole eggs
½ cup whole milk
1½ teaspoons Dijon mustard
6 everything bagel chips*
1 cup chopped spinach, divided
4 ounces smoked salmon, divided
Garnish: chopped chives

• Preheat oven to 350°. Grease 6 (½-cup) porcelain ramekins with cooking spray. Place on a rimmed baking sheet.
• In a medium bowl, stir together cream cheese, red onion, capers, and bagel seasoning.
• In another medium bowl, whisk together eggs, milk, and mustard.
• In prepared ramekins, layer the following: 1 bagel chip each, ½ cup spinach, 1 tablespoon cream cheese mixture each, 2 ounces smoked salmon, remaining ½ cup spinach, remaining cream cheese mixture, and remaining 2 ounces smoked salmon.
• Pour ¼ cup egg mixture into each ramekin. Let sit for 5 minutes. Tent ramekins with foil.
• Bake for 20 minutes. Remove foil, and bake until puffed and set, approximately 15 minutes more. Let cool for 10 minutes.
• Using a thin knife, loosen sides of stratas in each rame-kin. Invert each ramekin onto a small plate, bagel chip side up. Using a spatula, carefully flip over each strata, bagel chip side down, and transfer to a serving platter.
• Garnish with chives, if desired. Serve immediately.

We used New York Style Bagel Crisps.

MAKE-AHEAD TIP: Stratas can be assembled completely, covered, and refrigerated overnight. Tent with foil and bake just before serving.

Hash Brown Canapés

Makes 12

Filled with a delicious combination of Brie cheese, crumbled bacon, and Granny Smith apple, these petite potato cups are tasty and sophisticated morsels.

1 cup frozen shredded hash brown potatoes
¼ cup coarsely grated Parmesan cheese
¼ cup chopped green onion
2 teaspoons olive oil
¾ teaspoon fine sea salt, divided
¼ teaspoon ground black pepper
4 ounces Brie cheese, diced
3 strips bacon
1 cup diced Granny Smith apple
⅓ cup diced fennel
¼ cup diced red onion
1 tablespoon brown sugar
1 teaspoon apple cider vinegar
Garnish: fennel fronds

• Preheat oven to 400°. Grease a 12-well mini muffin pan with cooking spray.
• Line a rimmed baking sheet with paper towels. Place potatoes on prepared baking sheet and let thaw. Press all excess moisture out of potatoes.
• In a medium bowl, stir together thawed potatoes, Parmesan cheese, green onion, olive oil, ½ teaspoon salt, and pepper. Spoon 1½ tablespoons potato mixture into wells of prepared muffin pan. Press potato mixture into bottom and up sides of wells.
• Bake for 20 minutes. Add a Brie cheese piece to each potato cup. Bake until Brie melts and potato cups are crispy and golden brown, approximately 5 minutes more.
• Meanwhile, in a medium skillet, cook bacon over medium heat until crisp. Drain on paper towels. Crumble when cool. Reserve ½ teaspoon bacon grease in skillet. Add apple, fennel, red onion, brown sugar, vinegar, and remaining ¼ teaspoon salt. Sauté until soft and fragrant, 3 to 5 minutes.
• Gently remove potato cups from pan. Top each potato cup with crumbled bacon and apple mixture.
• Garnish with fennel fronds, if desired. Serve immediately.

1½ teaspoons fine sea salt, divided
½ teaspoon ground black pepper
1 medium butternut squash
¾ cup tri-color quinoa
1 large grapefruit
2 medium oranges
1 tablespoon chopped fresh mint
3 cups chopped, stemmed Russian kale
¼ cup chopped toasted walnuts
¼ cup pomegranate arils
Garnish: fresh mint

• Preheat oven to 400°.
• Using a sharp knife, trim and discard greens and roots from beets. Place beets in an 8-inch square baking dish. Add ¼ cup water, vinegar, 1 teaspoon olive oil, 1 teaspoon salt, and pepper, tossing to coat beets. Cover baking dish with foil.
• Bake beets until a paring knife can be inserted into beets without resistance, 30 to 35 minutes. Let cool completely. Peel and dice beets into ½-inch cubes.
• Peel and dice squash into ½-inch cubes. In a large bowl, toss together squash, 1 tablespoon olive oil, and remaining ½ teaspoon salt. Place in a single layer on a small rimmed baking sheet.
• Bake squash until slightly tender, 10 to 15 minutes. Let cool completely.
• In a medium saucepan, cook quinoa in remaining 1¼ cups water according to package instructions. Let cool completely.
• Using a sharp knife, peel and segment grapefruit and oranges, reserving ¼ cup juice. Chop grapefruit and orange segments into thirds.
• In a medium bowl, whisk together reserved ¼ cup citrus juice, mint, and remaining 1 tablespoon olive oil until emulsified. Add kale, tossing to coat.
• In 12 (6-ounce) trifle glasses, layer beets, kale, quinoa, grapefruit, orange, and squash. Top with walnuts and pomegranate arils. Serve immediately, or cover and refrigerate until needed, up to 3 hours. Serve cold or at room temperature.
• Garnish with mint, if desired.

MAKE-AHEAD TIP: Beets, squash, and quinoa can be cooked up to 2 days in advance. Let cool completely, place in individual airtight containers, and refrigerate until needed. Because layers may bleed into others, we recommend assembling and serving salads within 3 hours.

Layered Holiday Salads
Makes approximately 12

Colorful layers of beets, kale, butternut squash, quinoa, grapefruit, oranges, toasted walnuts, and pomegranate arils come together beautifully in this unique and nutritious holiday salad. If fresh mint isn't available, use 1 teaspoon dried mint or mint tea in the dressing instead.

6 baby red beets
1½ cups water, divided
2 tablespoons sherry vinegar
2 tablespoons plus 1 teaspoon olive oil, divided

Cherry Danish Christmas Tree

Makes approximately 16 servings

If there was ever a pastry that could double as a captivating centerpiece for your Christmas table, this is most certainly the one! Tree-shaped puff pastry filled with a cream cheese mixture and adorned with cherry "ornaments" and a light dusting of confectioners' sugar will undoubtedly delight your guests at first sight and with the first bite.

4 ounces cream cheese, softened
1 tablespoon eggnog
1 (17.3-ounce) box frozen puff pastry (2 sheets),
    thawed according to package directions
¼ cup cherry spreadable fruit*
1 egg, lightly beaten
½ cup pitted cherries
Garnish: confectioners' sugar

• Preheat oven to 400°. Line an 18x13-inch rimmed baking sheet with parchment paper.
• In a small bowl, whisk together cream cheese and eggnog.
• Unfold puff pastry sheets on a lightly floured surface. Using a rolling pin, roll out sheets to 13x11-inch rectangles.
• Transfer a puff pastry rectangle to prepared baking sheet. Using a knife, score a triangle with 11-inch-long sides and a 2-inch square at bottom for the Christmas tree and tree trunk into puff pastry rectangle.
• Spread cream cheese mixture over scored triangle, reserving ½ teaspoon mixture. Cover with second puff pastry sheet.**
• Using fingers, gently feel outline of cream cheese mixture. Using a sharp knife, score another 11-inch triangle with 2-inch square at bottom, matching Christmas tree outline of first puff pastry sheet as much as possible. (To avoid tearing parchment paper, press blade into puff pastry rather than sliding it.) Carefully trim away and reserve excess puff pastry from tree shape.
• Using a sharp knife, very lightly score ¾-inch-thick tree branches, following line of tree trunk. (Trunk should be wider near tree base and narrower at top.) Following the scored lines and pressing the knife blade straight down, cut branches into pastry tree.
• Working on one side of pastry tree at a time, gently peel back top puff pastry layer on each branch. Place a thin line of spreadable cherry on branches. Lightly press top and bottom puff pastry sheets together.

• Beginning at tree base, twist branches away from you. (Try to twist bottom branches twice.)
• Using a sharp knife or a star-shaped cutter, cut a star from puff pastry scraps. Place star on prepared baking sheet. Brush tree and star with egg.
• Bake until pastry is risen and golden brown, 12 to 15 minutes. (If tree trunk puffs too much during baking, pierce gently with a sharp knife.)
• Using a sharp knife, cut cherries in half. Using paper towels, blot cut sides of halved cherries to soak up extra liquid. Place halved cherries cut side down on puff pastry tree to resemble ornaments.
• Attach star to top of tree, using reserved ½ teaspoon cream cheese mixture as glue.
• Garnish with a dusting of confectioners' sugar, if desired. Serve immediately.

*We used Polaner All Fruit Spreadable Fruit.
**To keep second puff pastry from stretching while being moved, loosely roll up second puff pastry sheet jelly roll style. Line up roll with top of first puff pastry sheet and unroll puff pastry sheet to cover cream cheese mixture.

Cranberry-Lime Fruit Bread

Makes 1 (9x5-inch) loaf

This lovely loaf, studded with fresh cranberries and enriched with lime juice, is an appetizing canvas on which to devour our homemade Honey Butter. Serve this bake for brunch or give it as a gift.

1 large egg
½ cup vegetable oil
½ cup granulated sugar
½ cup light brown sugar

1 tablespoon fresh lime zest (approximately 2 large limes)
¼ cup fresh lime juice
½ cup whole buttermilk
2¼ cups all-purpose flour
1 teaspoon ground ginger
1 teaspoon baking soda
½ teaspoon baking powder
½ teaspoon fine sea salt
2 cups fresh cranberries
Honey Butter (recipe follows)

- Preheat oven to 350°. Spray a 9x5-inch loaf pan with baking spray with flour.
- In a large bowl, whisk together egg, oil, sugars, and lime zest and juice. Whisk in buttermilk.
- In a medium bowl, whisk together flour, ginger, baking soda, baking powder, and salt. Using a rubber spatula, fold flour mixture into egg mixture just until combined. Fold in cranberries. Pour batter into prepared pan. Using an offset spaulta, smooth top of batter, pushing batter into corners and sides of pan as necessary.
- Bake for 30 minutes. Tent pan with foil to prevent excessive browning. Bake until a wooden pick inserted in the center comes out clean, 30 minutes more.
- Let bread cool in pan on a wire rack for 20 minutes. Remove bread from pan, and let cool completely on a wire rack.
- Just before serving, slice bread and arrange on a serving platter or cake stand. Serve with Honey Butter.

Honey Butter
Makes ½ cup

This luscious spread—whether enjoyed on our Cranberry-Lime Fruit Bread or used for scones, biscuits, and more— is bound to become a favorite after just one taste.

½ cup unsalted butter, softened
1 tablespoon honey

- In a small bowl, stir together butter and honey until combined. Use immediately, or cover and refrigerate until needed. Let come to room temperature before using.

Tropical Oatmeal Cookies
Makes approximately 36

Laden with cardamom, shredded coconut, macadamia nuts, and dried mango, these toothsome cookies will remind you of a tropical vacation and are best accompanied by a cup of hot tea.

1 cup unsalted butter, softened
1 cup light brown sugar
1 cup granulated sugar
2 large eggs, room temperature
2 cups all-purpose flour
1 teaspoon baking soda
1 teaspoon fine sea salt
1 teaspoon ground cardamom

2½ cups quick-cooking oats
⅔ cup sweetened shredded coconut
⅔ cup chopped macadamia nuts
⅔ cup diced dried sweetened mango

- Preheat oven to 350°. Line several rimmed baking sheets with parchment paper.
- In a large mixing bowl, beat together butter and sugars with a mixer at high speed until light and fluffy. Add eggs, one at a time, beating well after each addition until incorporated.
- In a medium bowl, whisk together flour, baking soda, salt, and cardamom. Add flour mixture to butter mixture, beating until incorporated. With mixer at low speed, beat in oats, coconut, macadamia nuts, and mango until incorporated.
- Using a levered 1½-tablespoon scoop, drop dough 2 inches apart onto prepared baking sheets.
- Bake cookies until edges are golden brown, 12 to 14 minutes. Let cool on baking sheets for 3 minutes. Transfer cookies to wire racks. Let cool completely.

TEA-STEEPING *Guide*

The quality of the tea served at afternoon tea is as important as the food and the décor. To be sure your infusion is successful every time, here are some basic guidelines to follow.

WATER

Always use the best water possible. If the water tastes good, so will your tea. Heat the water on the stovetop or in an electric kettle to the desired temperature. A microwave oven is not recommended.

TEMPERATURE

Heating the water to the correct temperature is arguably one of the most important factors in making a pot of great tea. Pouring boiling water on green, white, or oolong tea leaves can result in a very unpleasant brew. Always refer to the tea purveyor's packaging for specific instructions, but in general, use 170° to 195° water for these delicate tea types. Reserve boiling (212°) water for black and puerh teas, as well as herbal and fruit tisanes.

TEAPOT

If the teapot you plan to use is delicate, warm it with hot tap water first to avert possible cracking. Discard this water before adding the tea leaves or tea bags.

TEA

Use the highest-quality tea you can afford, whether loose leaf or prepackaged in bags or sachets. Remember that these better teas can often be steeped more than once. When using loose-leaf tea, generally use 1 generous teaspoon of dry leaf per 8 ounces of water, and use an infuser basket. For a stronger infusion, add another teaspoonful or two of dry tea leaf.

TIME

As soon as the water reaches the correct temperature for the type of tea, pour it over the leaves or tea bag in the teapot, and cover the pot with a lid. Set a timer—usually 1 to 2 minutes for whites and oolongs; 2 to 3 minutes for greens; and 3 to 5 minutes for blacks, puerhs, and herbals. (Steeping tea longer than recommended can yield a bitter infusion.) When the timer goes off, remove the infuser basket or the tea bags from the teapot.

ENJOYMENT

For best flavor, serve the tea as soon as possible. Keep the beverage warm atop a lighted warmer or under your favorite tea cozy if necessary.

Acknowledgments

EDITOR Lorna Reeves
ART DIRECTOR Leighann Lott Bryant
ASSOCIATE EDITOR Katherine Ellis
SENIOR COPY EDITOR Rhonda Lee Lother
EDITORIAL ASSISTANT Shelby Duffy
SENIOR DIGITAL IMAGING SEPCIALIST
Delisa McDaniel

COVER

Photography by William Dickey • Photo Styling by Courtni Bodiford • Recipe Development/Food Styling by Jade Sinacori
Spode *Christmas Tree Gold Collection* teapot, teacup and saucer set, bread and butter plate, creamer and sugar set, and cake stand from Portmeirion, 888-778-1471, *portmeirion.com.* Gorham *Chantilly* flatware from Replacements, Ltd., 800-737-5223, *replacements.com.*

HOLIDAY GATHERING

Photography by John O'Hagan • Styling by Courtni Bodiford • Food Styling by Kathleen Kanen • Recipe Development by Janet Lambert
Pages 9–22: Lenox *Holiday* teapot, footed cup and saucer set, dinner plate, salad plate, water glasses, 13-inch chop plate, rectangular platter, 13-inch square platter, canapé tray, 10-inch oval fluted bowl, trivet, votive, and square condiment bowls; Lenox *Eternal* oval platter; Gorham *King Edward* flatware from Replacements, Ltd., 800-737-5223, *replacements.com.* Green napkins from World Market, 877-967- 5362, *worldmarket.com.* Location courtesy of Becky Jennings.

A HEALTHFUL CELEBRATION

Photography by Mac Jamieson • Styling by Courtni Bodiford • Food Styling by Katie Moon Dickerson and Megan Lankford • Recipe Development by Leah Rasbury and Vanessa Rocchio
Pages 23–34: Noritake *Colburn* teapot, creamer, covered sugar bowl, 11-inch oval serving platter, and 13-inch oval serving platter; Noritake *Limerick* creamer, covered sugar bowl, dinner plate, footed cup and saucer set, 2-tiered serving tray, and 3-tiered serving tray; Noritake *Palace Christmas Platinum Holiday* salad plate; Hutschenreuther *Revere* teapot and lid; Lunt Silver *Modern Victorian* teaspoon, salad fork, modern hollow knife, and demitasse spoon from Replacements, Ltd., 800-737-5223, *replacements.com.* Mercury glass candlesticks and gold stands from Hobby Lobby, 855-329-7060, *hobbylobby.com.* White table runner and napkins from HomeGoods, 833-888-0776, *homegoods.com.* Location courtesy of Byrom Building Corp.

VISIONS OF SNOWMEN

Photography by John O'Hagan • Photo Styling by Courtni Bodiford • Recipe Development/Food Styling by Jade Sinacori
Pages 35–46: Grace's Teaware *Snowman* teapot, creamer and sugar set, salad plates, teacup and saucer sets, and 3-tiered stand from The Twiggery, 800-979-8944, *thetwiggery.com.* Royal Doulton *Fontainebleau Green* dinner plates, bread and butter plates, and 13-inch oval platter; Cambridge Silver *Gold Royal Fashion* flatware from Replacements, Ltd., 800-737-5223, *replacements.com.* Frosted votives and plaid tablecloth overlay from Bed, Bath & Beyond, 800-462-3966, *bedbathandbeyond.com.* Snowman place card holders from Hobby Lobby, 800-888-0321, *hobbylobby.com.*

A COZY CHRISTMAS

Photography by John O'Hagan • Styling by Courtni Bodiford • Food Styling by Kellie Kelley • Recipe Development by Tricia Manzanero and Taylor Franklin Wann
Pages 47–56: Spode *Provincial Garden Cranberry* teapot,

creamer, covered sugar bowl, dinner plate, and mug and saucer set; Juliska *Country Estate Winter Holiday* ramekin; International Silver *Queen's Fancy* modern hollow knife, salad fork, and teaspoon from Replacements, Ltd., 800-737-5223, *replacements.com.* Juliska *Country Estate Winter Frolic* salad plate from Bromberg's, 205-871-3276, *brombergs.com.* Napkin rings from HomeGoods, 800- 888-0776, *homegoods .com.* Red-and-white buffalo check napkins available seasonally from Pottery Barn, 888-779-5176, *potterybarn.com.* Location courtesy of Bronwyn and Scot Cardwell.

GOLD & SILVER YULETIDE

Photography by Nicole Du Bois • Styling by Courtni Bodiford • Food Styling by Kathleen Kanen • Recipe Development by Tricia Manzanero and Taylor Franklin Wann
Pages 57–68: John Aynsley *Imperial Gold* teapot, creamer, sugar, salad plate, and footed cup and saucer set; Rosenthal *Monaco* charger; Royal Worcester *Hyde Park* dinner plate and cake plate; Royal Worcester *Imperial White* 12-inch chop plate and 15-inch and salad plate; Waterford Crystal *Kells* iced tea glass; Gorham Silver *Melrose* weighted pedestal cake stand; Gorham Silver *La Scala* modern hollow knife, salad fork, teaspoon, and demitasse spoon from Replacements, Ltd., 800-737-5223, *replacements.com.* Villeroy & Boch *Windsor* tablecloth and napkins; cake stand from HomeGoods, 800-888-0776, *homegoods.com.*

A VERY VEGAN CHRISTMAS

Photography by John O'Hagan • Styling by Courtni Bodiford • Food Styling by Vanessa Rocchio • Recipe Development by Laura Crandall and Becca Cummins
Pages 69–80: Mason's *Vista Blue* square gadroon teapot, large sandwich tray, square handled cake plate, 14-inch oval serving platter, and round fluted dessert bowl; Jones, George & Sons *Abbey* flat cup and saucer set; Booths *Real Old Willow Blue* creamer, covered sugar bowl, and dinner plate; Queen's *Seasons Greetings Blue* salad plate; Oneida Silver *Michelangelo* demitasse spoon, teaspoon, modern hollow knife, and salad fork; International Silver Royal Danish sterling napkin ring from Replacements, Ltd., 800-737-5223, *replacements.com.* Vine Floral Boutis round tablecloth from Williams Sonoma, 877-812-6235, *williams-sonoma.com.* Green Topiaries reversible gift wrap (discontinued) from The Enchanted Home, 800-804-9565, *enchantedhome.com.* Wreaths from Hobby Lobby, 855-329-7060, *hobbylobby.com.* Location courtesy of Kathleen Duquette.

HAPPY HOLIDAYS

Photography by John O'Hagan • Styling by Courtni Bodiford • Food Styling by Katie Moon Dickerson • Recipe Development by Janet Lambert
Pages 81–92: Herend *Golden Edge* teapot with rose; *Princess Victoria Green* teapot with rose; Chinese Bouquet Raspberry creamer, covered sugar bowl, and square cake plate with handles; *Chinese Bouquet Evergreen* oval platter and chop plate with handles; *Fish Scale Evergreen* dinner plate, teacup, saucer, oval platter, creamer, and covered sugar bowl from Herend, *herendusa.com.* American Atelier *Ornaments II* salad plate; Lunt Silver *Bel Chateau* hollow knife, teaspoon, and salad fork from Replacements, Ltd., 800-737-5223, *replacements.com.* Gold demitasse spoons, tablecloth, and Nicole Miller table runner from HomeGoods, 833-888-0776, *homegoods.com.* Green napkins from World Market, 877-967-5362, *worldmarket.com.* Miniature mercury tree and ornaments from Target, 800-440-0680, *target.com.* Green velvet trees and green mercury trees from Hobby Lobby, 855-329-7060, *hobbylobby.com.*

COOKIES FOR SANTA

Photography by Stephanie Welbourne Steele • Styling by Melissa Sturdivant Smith • Recipe Development/Food Styling by Anita Simpson Spain

Pages 93–104: Fitz & Floyd *Winter Holiday Santa* teapot; Fitz & Floyd *St. Nicholas* flat cup and saucer set, dinner plate, salad plate, bread and butter plate, creamer, covered sugar bowl, 14-inch oval serving platter, and 10-inch diameter pedestal cake stand from Replacements, Ltd., 800-737-5223, *replacements.com.* Kurt S. Adler gingerbread claydough house from Wayfair, 844-378-4513, *wayfair.com.*

TEA FOR CHRISTMASTIDE

Photography by William Dickey • Photo Styling by Courtni Bodiford • Recipe Development/Food Styling by Jade Sinacori
Pages 105–116: Spode *Christmas Tree Grove* dinner plates, salad plates, 17-inch rectangular serving platter, and 9-inch square bowl; Gorham *Chantilly* flatware from Replacements, Ltd., 800-737-5223, *replacements.com.* Spode *Christmas Tree* bread and butter plates and teacup and saucer sets; Spode *Christmas Tree Gold Collection* teapot, teacup and saucer set, creamer and sugar set, and cake stand from Portmeirion, 888-778-1471, *portmeirion.com.* Ceriart ivory scalloped platter and Belmont Collection tablecloth and napkin set from HomeGoods, 800- 888-0776, *homegoods.com.* Centerpiece by FlowerBuds, 205-970-3223, *flowerbuds floristbirmingham.com.*

A FESTIVE BRUNCH

Photography by John O'Hagan • Styling by Lucy Finney • Food Styling by Kathleen Kanen • Recipe Development by J. R. Jacobson
Pages 117–128: Mackenzie-Childs *Evergreen* (discontinued) enamel dinner plate, salad plate, and compote; *Courtly Check* enamel 4-cup teapot, saucer, and napkin rings from Mackenzie-Childs, 888-665-1999, *mackenzie-childs.com.* Mackenzie-Childs *Courtly Check* enamel little sugar bowl, creamer, and teacup from Christine's on Canterbury, 205-871-8297.

EDITOR'S NOTE: Items not listed are from private collections and no further information is available.

DARK CHOCOLATE–PEPPERMINT COOKIES (page 115)

Piping Guide

Pipe on all 2½" lines within the 12½" x 16"

AMBROSIA CAKES,
page 19

CRANBERRY & CHERRY-TOPPED
CHEESECAKES,
page 21

Recipe Index

EDITOR'S NOTE: Recipe titles shown in red are gluten-free, provided gluten-free versions of processed ingredients (such as flours and extracts) are used.